D1503177

How to Develop

The Successful Pitcher

Ron Squire

Baseball Coach
Mt. San Antonio College
California

♦ ♦ ♦ ♦

How to Develop

The Successful Pitcher

♦ ♦ ♦ ♦

Prentice-Hall, Inc.
Englewood Cliffs, N. J.

Second printing ....February, 1967

DEDICATED TO

My father, Russel N. Squire and *my college coach, John Scolinos,*
whose inspiration, assistance, and patience made this book possible.

♦ The Key to Winning Baseball

Of the nine men on a baseball team, the pitcher bears the greatest responsibility for the outcome of the game. From the majors on down through little league, the situation is the same . . . a team without good pitching is most often a losing team. It follows, then, that the most important facet of a coach's job is developing winning pitchers. In professional ball, the problem is primarily one of scouting and selecting. Who is ready to do the job now or where can we get the type pitcher we need for the job? Below the majors, the problem is usually how the coach is going to find anyone who can pitch at all. The answer to this problem is that the coach many times must develop his own pitchers . . . from scratch if necessary.

Whether the coach is a college coach, a high school coach, an interested father, or a little league coach, the important thing to realize is that *pitching can be taught*. Seldom is a pitcher self-made. It is the coaches job to help the pitcher make his fast ball move and his curve break. The knowledge of how to help the pitcher develop successfully is the key to being a winning coach.

Usually acquiring this knowledge is an arduous process of playing, studying, and coaching the game over a period of years. *How to Develop the Successful Pitcher* was written to short-cut the process. It may be used as a step-by-step process in the development of the pitcher or may be referred to as a means of solving specific problems or developing specific skills for the individual pitcher. The book is organized so the reader can turn to a certain page and find out how to analyze, diagnose, and remedy, his particular problem.

The basic pitches are covered—the fast ball and the curve—

7

in separate chapters and a chapter on specialty pitches for the exceptional pitcher is included. Other points covered range from the attitude and conditioning of the winning pitcher, through form and delivery, to control and strategy, with the more subtle points of setting up hitters described in easy to understand rules.

I realize that there is no one way of doing things, but I feel that this book holds answers to every important question and problem a coach will run into. Many of the ideas are mine, but many of them were picked up over the years in conversations with other coaches and major league players, and from clinics and research.

How to Develop the Successful Pitcher would not have been possible without the valuable assistance of many people. I am indebted to Ed Bressoud, Don Rowe, John Scolinos, and Russel Squire for their careful criticisms and suggestions in preparing the manuscript, and to William C. Squire who spent many hours drawing the illustrations. A special thanks is due my wife, Shirley, who prepared the entire manuscript and patiently helped in the proofreading.

For the real reward in coaching, an association with many loyal and hard-working young men, I thank the players I have been privileged to coach.

◆ Contents

9

How to Develop
The Successful Pitcher

♦ Creating a Successful
Pitching Environment

Pitching is a skill that can be learned. Given a boy with minimum physical abilities and the desire to learn, and the capable coach can help him develop into a successful pitcher. Both the pitcher and the coach must believe this. We are all looking for the pitcher with the overpowering fast ball. This is truly an important gift, but it will not assure the player success. Nor will the young pitcher who finds himself without this gift be doomed to defeat.

Good pitchers are successful because they are *pitchers*, not throwers. A good thrower can become a good pitcher, but it is a long difficult trip with the coach acting as guide and the pitcher working hard to follow instructions.

This book will cover the trip from beginning to end, anticipating the road blocks and trials along the way. Success and a grand feeling of accomplishment for both coach and pitcher are the rewards. But remember, the coach cannot *"learn"* the boy how to pitch, he can only aid him in learning.

This relationship between the coach and pitcher must be established early in the process. There will be much experimenting along the way, and without full cooperation efficiency will be hindered. To gain the pitcher's cooperation the coach must have something to offer. He must be prepared, and have the necessary knowledge, to help the pitcher. When the coach is constructively helping his pitchers along the route to success, he should not have to worry about demanding respect from them or dealing with disciplinary problems. The coach who does not have the knowledge to help his pitchers is in trouble from the start. Respect and cooperation are *earned*, not *demanded*.

It is important that the pitcher and coach embark upon the "trip" with confidence in each other; and both must be filled with a burning desire to succeed. As no one is *born* with "pitching-coach" knowledge, the coach must strive continuously to gain more information and to find ways of imparting this information to his pitchers. Just as pitching can be learned by the willing boy, knowledge can also be acquired by the conscientious coach. It is his obligation to acquire this knowledge and get it across to his pitchers. It is the pitcher's obligation to assimilate this information and to work untiringly to perfect his skills. Together, as a team, success will be reached.

There is more to developing the successful pitcher than teaching him the basic fundamentals. An environment must be established that breeds success. The New York Yankees have such an environment. Their organization has done much to spur its players to greater heights of achievement.

The successful environment is no accident; its seed must be planted and nourished carefully. In cultivating this environment, no detail is too small to consider. As an example, the way the pitcher walks on and off the mound is revealing of the pride, confidence, poise, and general tone of success that prevails on the entire staff. The coach may even have to teach his pitchers how to walk.

This chapter will tell how to establish the successful environment, the prime requisite for success. Do not overlook its importance, it is not easily come by. Trying to develop a pitcher in a poor environment is like trying to build a house on the sand.

DEVELOPING SUCCESSFUL ATTITUDES IN THE PITCHER

Successful attitudes must be built from the ground up. As coach you must be conscious of this the very first time you work with a new player, because a pitcher's outlook is nearly as important as his abilities. That is why a mediocre pitcher with a confident approach can often beat the gifted one with the defeatist attitude.

Willingness to learn

A pitching prospect must be open-minded and eager to learn. This is not always a natural beginning and many times the coach must work at implanting them in the boy.

Enlist the cooperation of the parents when starting to work with a new pitcher. Explain to them what you and the boy hope to accomplish. Let the mother in on it, too. Use the father to help the boy with drills at home, and give him plenty of credit for developing the boy as far as he has. Invite the parents of your pitchers to a meeting and explain your over-all program to them. Let them know the attitudes you are trying to develop and the skills you are trying to teach. Without the parents' cooperation the path ahead will be difficult indeed.

Learning to pitch is a gradual process. Do not tear the beginner apart and try to change him overnight. Watch him pitch and let him do the talking in the beginning. Sell the young pitcher on the fact that you are interested in helping him. He must first feel the need for this help. Do not push yourself upon him. You might say, "You have the makings of a fine curve ball, maybe if you held it more loosely it might break even better." Make sure it will! Your first instruction must meet with success, as you are striving to do no more at this time than to get acquainted and gain the boy's confidence.

The pitcher must recognize that you are leaving no stone

unturned in your effort to help him toward his goal. The day will come when he will *ask* you for help. The *real* learning process is then ready to begin. The pitcher is now open-minded and eager to learn through his own choice. The work ahead is difficult but now you have a chance of succeeding.

Pride

Webster's Dictionary gives several interesting definitions of pride: one of these is, "a sense of one's own dignity or worth;" another, certainly related to our building of a successful environment, "the best of a class, group, society, etc.: as, the *pride* of the Yankees." Throughout the building of the environment and during the instruction, you are instilling in your pitchers the concept that they are going to be successful because they are working hard and efficiently and are members of an organization that breeds success.

Pride is not composed of over-confidence and conceit. It is the process of being proud of the hard work entailed, the fundamentals mastered, the victories gained, and the lessons learned from defeat. Pride allows the pitcher to learn from defeat and spurs him on to use these lessons to succeed the next time.

To help develop this pride a tradition must be built. Nothing builds tradition like success. If you have had successful pitchers in the past, use this to instill pride in your present staff. Have the old pitchers come back and talk with the new ones. Demonstrate that you have pride in your pitchers by sticking up for them in public and praising them when they deserve it. Help your pitchers to their successes, but do not take credit for them.

Confidence

The pitcher has confidence when he knows he is well prepared. Confidence is a positive ingredient that the pitcher has worked for. It is not a hollow word to him, nor is it the act of putting on a phony front. He has worked hard to master his skills and is ready to bank this hard work on getting the batter out. You can help develop this confidence by letting your pitcher know that you would not be working with him if you did not feel that he was going to be a success.

In our locker room are several signs depicting the type of confidence we are striving to build. "Our pitchers have confidence because they have mastered the mechanics and knowledge to be successful." "Success, not pep-talks, breeds confidence." A general idea of the part confidence plays on a successful pitching staff might be represented by the following statement made by one of our pitchers. "I have a good chance of getting the opposing batter out because I have worked harder for perfection than the batter and stake all this time and effort on getting the batter out." When the pitcher really believes this, he *has* confidence.

Confidence in any situation is knowing that you have the ability and knowledge to cope with the situation. It is our belief that this is developed in young pitchers by facing every conceivable game situation over and over again until the solution is second nature. Practice should be geared to afford pitchers the opportunities to cope with these situations. This segment of building confidence is treated thoroughly in the next chapter. The coach must be careful to match the situation to the pitcher's own level of ability so that confidence is built, not destroyed. Confidence is built through positive action and practice, not through talking.

Poise

In many locker rooms throughout the country the inscription "Keep Your Poise," is written. Poise merits this importance because it is an outward manifestation of pride and confidence which a successful pitcher must possess.

The pitcher can demonstrate his poise in many ways. He should walk out to the mound showing that he means business. Some pitchers look as if they were sneaking up on the mound. When a batter sees one of these timid souls taking the hill, it makes him feel like a hitter.

The pitcher should take his warmup throws in an efficient manner and then "take charge" of the situation. He should have a look of confidence and assurance as he receives his sign. When the inning is over he must get off the mound and back to the dugout in a brisk manner. We recommend that pitchers practice walking on and off the field. In general, they should be taught how to act on the mound—and off. It will pay dividends in developing the over-all "class" of your staff.

If the pitcher or another team member makes an error, the pitcher should not show his concern, but should go on with the business of getting the next batter out. This will tend to bolster the confidence of the whole team and will not let the opposition detect a weakness in his armor. There is nothing more disconcerting than to hit a home run and have the pitcher look as if he did not even see it. If, on the other hand, he slams his glove down or kicks the dirt, the opposition know they "have" him. There is plenty of time for the pitcher to let the next batter know he means business without kicking dirt all over the rubber.

Some days one pitch may be working better than another. If the curve is not working well the pitcher should go with his other pitches until his curve begins to perform. Many pitchers who lack poise, under the same situation, will kick the dirt, cry all over the mound, and let everybody in the ball park know their curve is not working. This pitcher is a loser.

It is important that the uniform be neat and be worn properly. We always have the shoes shined, the sanitaries clean, and the hair cut short. These may be trivial matters but they add up when it comes to appraising the complete poise or "class" of the successful pitcher. A successful pitcher should *look* like a successful pitcher.

Willingness to sacrifice

To become a successful pitcher the boy must be willing to pay the price. Anything worth acquiring costs something. The boy must be acquainted with this from the very beginning. Two dedicated pitchers willing to pay the price are better than a dozen boys making a half-hearted attempt. We always point out to prospective pitchers that if it were easy to become a pitcher, major league pitchers would not be paid $50,000 a year.

Desire and hustle

When we speak of desire we do not mean the jumping-up-and-down, hand-clapping type often exhibited by football crowds. Many times this type of action is just noise on the surface and we refer to it as *false hustle*. The desire and hustle we are interested in are tied up with *pride, confidence*, and *poise*. It is the burning inner desire to be the best at whatever one is attempting. The "harder-I-get-hit-the-harder-I'll-throw type pitcher," may think he is fooling everybody into thinking he has great desire, but he is only fooling himself. A pitcher with real desire and hustle will step back, figure out what he is doing wrong and proceed to map out a course of retaliation. There is no time for play-acting or false hustle on the mound.

Many young pitchers exhibit this false hustle because they feel it is the thing to do, but this kind of action draws away from their efficiency. Real desire is exhibited by the pitcher who is thinking every second and working toward getting that man with the bat out of there. If the pitcher does this, he does not have to explain how much desire he has. The pitcher should exhibit his desire by doing his best to get the batter out while he is on the mound not by showing how hard he can kick the dugout when he has been relieved.

Desire begins when the boy reports to his first practice—and never ends. He is always striving for excellence. If the pitcher does not hustle in every practice (think, work, and sweat to the maximum) he will never be a successful pitcher. We do not commend a boy for desire and hustle—we *expect* it of him.

Pitcher's job on the bench

Each pitcher should be assigned a specific duty to perform during the game. Each one of these jobs is important to the team and also helps the pitcher's mental development. The assignment of specific duties also keeps the staff on its toes and does away with bickering which many times results when pitchers have nothing to do. The major duties are as follows:

1. Charting. Our pitchers and hitters and the opposition's pitchers and hitters.
2. Observing opposing batters.
3. Observing our batters.
4. Observing the opposing pitcher for tip-offs, weaknesses, strengths, set patterns, *etc.*

On several occasions we have knocked an opposing pitcher from the box because one of our bench pitchers was alert enough to discover the pitcher was tipping one of his pitches. By having everyone on the bench working hard, team morale is kept at a high level.

Readiness to pitch

The pitcher on the bench with the sour, frowning look, or the one who evades your glance everytime you are about to call upon him, is not likely to ever be of much help. The pitcher on the bench must be alert and be thinking with the game. He must be ready at a moment's notice to do a good job. From the pitcher's standpoint, he may not get many chances to prove himself and must be ready to go when the occasion arises. We have had pitchers who sat and sulked on the bench, and then when finally called upon, failed, because they were not mentally prepared. On the other hand, the pitcher who is ready, may do a superb job and the other pitchers may never get him off the mound. We do not want our pitchers to be content with sitting on the bench, but we do expect them to do their jobs and be mentally ready when called upon.

MAKING THE BEST USE OF AVAILABLE PERSONNEL

It is said of many winning coaches that they win because they always have the horses. To a great extent the coach can exert an important influence upon the number and quality of the horses he gets each year. Through efficient organization he can minimize the familiar cry of the losing coach, "I just never have the material to win." The solution is to stimulate as much interest as possible in the program so that many pitchers try out, and then to efficiently organize the program so that none of the material is wasted. It is the coach's responsibility to build his stable of horses.

Feeder teams

Feeder teams are an important foundation upon which to build a successful pitching environment. This foundation usually consists of the junior high, elementary, and youth baseball programs within the community. The high school coach should aid the coaches on these levels to develop their pitchers and should also show a keen personal interest in their development.

Interest can be stimulated by holding clinics in cooperation with the personnel of these various groups. In these clinics, fundamentals that can be stressed at these levels should be presented and the over-all program should be sold to players and coaches alike.

Some provision should be made for these groups to see the varsity games. The varsity pitchers should meet these young boys and help them become a part of this contagious, successful environment. Success breeds success, so the coach should provide every opportunity for it to rub off on others.

An information sheet on the prospects who are pitching for these various groups should be prepared in cooperation with the coaches at these levels.

Organization within the school

The organization within the school should be set up with the purpose of taking care of as many pitchers as possible. The ideal situation is not to have to "cut" any of them. If they are willing to put out the effort to become pitchers they should be afforded the opportunity to do so. It is not always possible to have a program large enough to accommodate everyone, although there are some schools that have as many as six baseball teams. Methods of taking care of those that are cut are discussed in the next section.

The organization should be functional so that a boy knows that he has a chance to move up to the next spot if he improves and conversely, the boys on top must remain alert or the ones below will take their positions. The coaches of the various teams must work together to make sure the teaching is consistent and that the skills are taught and learned in a logical progression.

To better define the aspects of a successful organization the following hypothetical organization is presented. Although every school presents different problems, the underlying principles remain the same. This school has approximately two thousand students, half of them boys. It is a four-year high school consisting of grades nine through twelve.

There are four baseball teams, ninth grade, junior varsity reserve, junior varsity, and varsity. Only ninth graders can play on the ninth grade team. The ninth grade pitchers work mainly on control and proper techniques of throwing the fast ball. Basic fundamentals are stressed in the ninth grade with little emphasis upon winning. The junior varsity reserve team consists of tenth and eleventh graders who cannot make the junior varsity or varsity teams. This is the weakest group and provides for those less proficient pitchers who still have the desire to learn. The junior varsity team consists of the most talented tenth and eleventh graders. Second year pitchers (usually tenth graders) in this group perfect their over-all delivery and begin work on their curve. Third year (usually eleventh grade) pitchers perfect their breaking pitches and fast balls and work on their change-of-pace.

The varsity consists of any grade level pitcher proficient enough to make it. Five to seven pitchers are carried on the varsity, five to seven on the ninth grade team, four on the junior varsity with the reserves handling as many as are left over.

The techniques recommended for stress, on each level, are only illustrative of the fact that there should be progression between levels. The pitcher should certainly be encouraged to advance at his own rate. Throughout this book, progression is described in the teaching of each skill so this should not be a problem.

At first glance, you may feel that this organization would not be practical for your situation. This may be partially true, as no two situations are alike. The underlying principles of this organization will, however, help you to build the successful environment. This could hold true on the junior college and college levels as well. This hypothetical organization is suggested to better illustrate how these principles might be worked into a program. As a further aid to the coach, the basic principles involved are listed below:

1. The program should be organized to include as many pitchers as possible.
2. Every pitcher should be afforded the opportunity to learn if he so desires.
3. There should be a progression of skills taught.
4. The coach should be assigned to the team for which his ability best suits him.
5. The organization must be functional so that pitchers can move up or down the ladder freely.
6. The same philosophy and spirit of pride and success must be stressed at all levels.
7. Each coach must keep a careful evaluation of the progress of his pitchers.
8. The coaching staff as well as the pitching staff must work as a unit in striving for success.
9. No boy in the program should be slighted, because some boys mature later than others, or learn more slowly than others. Today's failure may well become tomorrow's success.

Organization of the overflow

As previously mentioned, many school organizations find it impossible to handle all the pitchers that try out for the teams and some have to be dropped. This is unfortunate and is certainly not recommended.

The coach can help these boys continue their pursuit of pitching prowess by getting them on community sponsored teams. If these teams do not already exist civic minded citizens willing and able to help in the program can usually be found.

An intramural program may also be set up to encourage these boys to continue playing ball. We have found many times that a boy who was too small or inexperienced in the ninth grade but who has stuck with it, has developed into a fine pitcher by his senior year. You should leave no stone unturned in finding places for these boys to play.

The summer program

In the summer these boys should be brought back into the instructional program for further development. The summer instructional program is very important in the development of the pitcher. It is a time when a pitcher can experiment and work on new techniques without the pressure of time, or the pressure of having to win the next day. It is also a period when the pitcher can work on such a phase of the program as strength development.

In organizing the summer program an ample amount of time should be set aside for instruction periods. In most communities there are many teams that the pitcher can join. It is recommended that he only pitch one game a week and reserve the rest of the time for instruction, development, and experimentation. The pitcher should be free to try these new techniques in the actual games during the summer, as an example, we sometimes tell our pitchers that they must throw at least three change-up pitches an inning during the summer. This is the only way we have of getting them to gain confidence in this type pitch under actual game conditions.

Tryouts and ratings

The boys whom we are discussing when speaking of tryouts are those pitchers new to the school or prospects we have seen before, whom we want to evaluate more completely. The pitchers already a part of the system have been quite thoroughly evaluated, and their tryout period, so to speak, will be their performance in the regular practice later on.

The tryout period can be a traumatic experience for the candidates and a waste of time for the coach, if it is not handled correctly. The candidates should be notified at least three weeks in advance of the impending tryouts. This will give them time to get their arms in shape and give ample time for information to be passed out regarding the tryouts.

The organizer should keep in mind at what levels the pitchers may be used. A ninth grader should not be compared with a senior, for example. On the first day of tryouts, the pitchers should be segregated as nearly as possible according to their respective grade levels and general levels of ability. It is much easier to evaluate the pitchers when they are divided in this manner.

Each coach will evaluate each pitcher and then the coaches will get together and compare their evaluations. Any information from previous tryouts or from former coaches is considered in the final evaluation. It is important to be as objective as possible in evaluating the prospect. By having each coach make a separate evaluation the judgment is more nearly accurate and fair.

The tryout should not be a one-day, do-or-die proposition. Some boys will be very nervous and will perform far below their actual ability. We want to find out what pitching aptitude each candidate actually possesses. What he does under pressure is not of interest to us at this time. We want to know if he possesses the minimum essentials for becoming a successful pitcher. Only time will tell whether he has the hard-to-measure mental capabilities, inner fortitude, desire, and the many other ingredients that go into the make-up of the successful pitcher.

There are few pitchers that can perform well with a coach standing behind them writing everything down on a clip board. The coaches should make the atmosphere of the tryouts as friendly as possible and show the candidates that they are interested in them as human beings not just as puppets.

The first day of observation, general notes can be made about each pitcher concerning his height, weight, length of arms, size of hands, and over-all delivery. These observations are made rather casually as the boys are pitching easily to their catchers.

After practice these general notes are transferred to regular forms.

SAMPLE

PITCHER INFORMATION SHEET

Name .... Age .... Grade ....
Height .... Weight .... Body Build ....
Hands .... Probable Level of Ability ....
Type Delivery .... Recommend Change of Delivery? ......
Fielding Ability ...... General Athletic Ability...... Poise .....
Desire ...... Fast ball ...... Comments ....
....
....
Curve ball .... Comments ....
....
Change-of-Pace .... Comments ....
Other Pitches .... Comments ....
Outstanding Strengths ....
....
....
Weaknesses ....
....
General Comments ....
....
....

The second day, after warming up, the pitcher's fielding drill is used to find out how each boy moves and to get an indication of his athletic ability. (Refer to drill number twenty on page 204). By the end of this second day, after having observed the pitchers for approximately forty-five minutes each day, you will have a general notion of which boys have a chance to become pitchers.

The next two days are spent in rating the pitchers' different pitches and general ability. You should also endeavor to find out something about the boy's willingness to work, his desire, and his capability to learn. You must be careful about judging learning capacity as some boys give the impression of being slow learners when they actually are not.

The fast ball should be judged on how well it moves. Does it hop or tail off? Is it a *live* fast ball? Breaking pitches should be judged on their *rotation* i.e., the spin of the ball. Does the curve rotate *downward* or is it *flat?* Does it break sharply, or does it hang? *Control* must also be checked as the different pitches are thrown.

It may look like a simple task to rate the pitchers' different pitches. It would be, if that is all you had to do. One question to be answered is, does his fast ball fail to "hop" and his curve fail to "break" because he has poor pitching aptitude, or because he is going about it in the wrong way? If the latter is true, he may still be a prospect. Objective type answers to specific questions as shown on the sample form are important as far as they go, but you still have to make the decision whether you think the boy ever has a chance of becoming a successful pitcher.

If his arm is adequate, his coordination acceptable, and he seems willing to learn, *give him a chance.* You will find in a four- or five-day tryout, following the methods prescribed, that you will not miss very often. In the final analysis, go over the objective data and information supplied from the forms, look over any past information that might be available, and with your coaching staff as a group, decide to keep him if there is any possibility that he might become a successful pitcher. Look for reasons to keep him, not reasons to drop him; mistakes then will be kept at a minimum.

Developing proper attitudes and establishing a sound organization is certainly an important step along the road to developing the successful pitcher. The firm base for our operation has been established. We are now ready to find out how an eager and willing thrower placed in a successful environment can be developed into a successful pitcher.

◆ Proper Techniques
For Instructing the Pitcher

two

The successful environment, the framework within which the coach and pitcher are going to work has been carefully established. The next step on the road to pitching success is of utmost importance. The coach must know how to get the best from his pitching prospects. A coach may know all there is to know about the curve ball, but if he does not understand pitching readiness, methods of motivation, and ways of getting his techniques across, his knowledge about the curve ball is of little value. He is like the pitcher with great "stuff" who cannot get it over. This is the reason great ball players do not necessarily make great coaches. In this chapter we shall tell how to handle different levels of ability, how to match teaching techniques to mental and physical aptitudes, how to adjust to physical limitations, and how to motivate the pitcher. We shall also present many teaching techniques to be used on each level.

PITCHING READINESS

A coach will receive pitchers at various stages of development, representing various levels of ability. It must first be determined at which level to begin the instruction. The pitcher cannot simply be classified beginner, intermediate, and advanced, because no two pitchers are at exactly the same level of development. Do not try to force a level of achievement upon a player. Asserting that all junior pitchers should have mastered the "get-it-in-there" curve and should now be working on the "extra" curve would be a fallacy. You must work with each pitcher on the level that he has reached.

In the following section we shall recommend a progression of pitching skills purely as a guide to aid in setting up the program of instruction. Although the progressions recommended will not meet the needs of all pitchers, it can be used as a guide in setting up a plan for individual boys.

Recommended progression of pitching skills

In establishing the successful environment it was recommended that you start developing the pitchers at the junior high level (seventh and eighth grade level). The aspiring pitching candidate should only throw fast balls at this level. He should be helped to iron out any flaws in his delivery and he must work on the most important aspect of pitching—*control*. He can be taught the rudiments of fielding his position, keeping his arm in shape, and thinking and acting like a pitcher.

Before the candidate enters the ninth grade the coach and the boy should make a study of his pitching and determine what his needs are now. Ways of determining his needs are discussed in a following chapter. The pitcher is now ready to begin learning the basic fundamentals of the curve ball. Care must be taken that this beginning instruction is correct, because wrong habits learned now will be hard to undo later on. The curve ball learned at this stage should be practiced over and over until the young pitcher is confident that he can throw it for a strike. The actual step-by-step procedure is presented in the chapter dealing specifically with teaching the curve ball.

The pitcher should work on his mastery of the curve and his fast ball during his ninth grade year. He should strive to throw his pitches down the pipe rather than try to hit the corners or be fancy. You must be careful to keep in mind the welfare of the pitcher's arm and not over-do his work-out periods at this time. Be patient. The attitudes developed now will be setting the tone for the rest of the young pitcher's career. Do not push too hard. Remember, the coach *helps* the pitcher develop, he cannot do the developing for him.

When the pitcher has good control of his fast ball and curve he can begin work on his change-of-pace; first, off the fast ball, and then off the curve ball. The pitcher who has mastered these pitches is well on his way. He should then work to perfect an "extra" fast ball or an "extra" curve. These pitches are in contrast to his "get-it-in-there" pitches developed earlier. The amount of time spent on each pitch depends on how fast the pitcher learns. Some may not advance past learning the curve while others will get as far as the "extra" pitches by the time they graduate from high school.

Matching teaching techniques to meet mental aptitudes

The pitching coach will be dealing with boys of varying mental capacities. He must determine which are the slow learners and which learn more quickly. It is useless to use every teaching aid when *one* would suffice. If the pitcher is a slow learner the problem may have to be approached from many different angles before the point is made. Resourcefulness and imagination are important. The pitcher with the lower I.Q. has a chance to reach the same level of competence as the boy with the higher I.Q., although it may take a little longer and their paths may vary. The fast learner may be able to learn through abstract word pictures and analogies while the slow learner will learn more easily from the sense of feel. The most successful coaches are those that understand these differences in capabilities and have the know how to present their instruction from many different angles and many different levels. Throughout this book different ways of teaching the pitching skills are presented. With some pitchers you may have to try them all.

Matching teaching techniques to meet physical aptitudes

While coaches have to adjust to mental differences they also have to make allowances for physical differences. A physical diagnosis of the pitchers must be made. In the first chapter the ways of doing this were presented. We can not expect all the pitchers to act the same way any more than we can expect them all to think the same way.

The tall, lean, over-hand pitcher, with the good fast ball should grip the ball across the seams to give it back spin and thus produce a "hopping" fast ball. The short stubby pitcher might be better off gripping it with the seams and a little off center to make it sink. Some pitchers will have better curve ball potential than others. Some experts feel that those pitchers with short, stubby fingers can not throw the curve as well as those with long tapering fingers. Be careful of such generalizations—although they may serve as a clue for judging future capabilities. Experiment in order to find out what is best for each pitcher. Guard against stereotyping the pitcher too early in his career as it is best to let him develop naturally in the beginning. Do not disregard the pitchers' physical abilities nor expect the same level of performance from each one. Develop an individual plan for making the best use of their capabilities.

Over-coaching

Many of us, in our enthusiasm to do a good job, are guilty of over-coaching. Coaches should not attempt to change a young pitcher's technique just for the sake of change. Many proven pitchers have individual idiosyncrasies in their deliveries and to change them might ruin their effectiveness. The correction of bad habits and the proper development of sound fundamentals are very important but you must be sure that what you are doing is actually helping the pitcher. You are not guilty of poor coaching just because in any particular movement you have no correction to make. This might be compared to the man at a party who feels he is a social misfit if he is not talking every second. There is a time in coaching to listen and to observe.

Do not try to give the young pitcher too much, too soon. Be content to work on a little bit at a time. If the pitcher is over-coached he will soon become discouraged. Let him plod along feeling his own way. *Be patient!*

METHODS OF MOTIVATION

Motivation is an important aspect of any learning situation; it is the driving force behind achievement. Man's motives are many, and the successful coach will take advantage of these to stimulate the development of his pitchers. The greater the motivation the greater the learning. There are many underlying principles of motivation. It is not within the framework of this book to discuss all of these principles. We will, instead, present some of the practical methods coaches might employ to better stimulate their pitcher's learning.

The environment and motivation

Once a successful environment is established a large step has been taken in motivating the pitchers. When competition for team membership is high, motivation to improve is increased. There is nothing harder than trying to motivate a pitcher who already knows he is the only pitcher in school. If this is the case the pitcher should be motivated to become the best in the league or the state. The bait should be just out of reach so that the pitcher will always be striving to improve. The skill that is being taught however, must be within the reach of the pitcher. It is true, he must have an *inner* desire to succeed; but the environment, and methods of motivation used by the coach, can help strengthen this desire.

The young pitcher is forever seeking status. You can help him recognize that status can be gained through becoming an outstanding pitcher.

The environment can be enhanced by staging rallies, gaining adequate coverage in the papers and stimulating interest among the parents. Worthy of mention is the forming of a girls' baseball appreciation club. The club can be organized to explain the inner workings of baseball and some of the basic rules. You should meet with this club at least once a week. The girls usually are interested in purchasing sweat shirts with the school name on them and they should show up in mass at all the ball games. In general, at the high school level, where the girls go, the boys will go. Thus the crowds at the game will become larger and interest will run higher. The purpose of attempting to stimulate this great interest is to make attainment of success more important to the player. Recognition is a great motivational force upon the young pitcher.

Praise and reward

Praise, satisfaction, and reward are more valuable than such negative factors as punishment and discomfort. It is a good general rule to end each day's work-out with some successful action. Praise must be earned, the pitchers know when the praise is insincere. Unfounded praise does more harm than good.

Failure

Some amount of failure is inevitable. The boy must realize that through meeting failure, understanding it, and doing one's best to conquer it, comes success. The pitcher must understand *why* he failed in order to improve. If the pitcher curves the hitter on three and two with the bases loaded and the hitter hits it out of the ball park, the pitcher should know why it happened. The following analysis could be made from this hypothetical situation: (1) the curve hung; therefore, the pitcher either released it too soon, did not bend his back, did not follow through, or did not snap his wrist; (2) the hitter was a curve ball hitter and was looking for the curve; therefore, it was the wrong pitch to throw; (3) the pitcher tipped his pitch; therefore, he will have to correct this fault and; (4) the pitch broke well on the low outside corner which was the hitter's weakness; therefore, the pitcher did not fail, the batter did an outstanding job of succeeding. Many more observations might be made in a situation such as this. There is always a reason for failure. If it is understood much can be gained from failure. In instance number four the pitcher did not fail at all although at the time the pitcher's failure to perform seemed obvious. Failure must be understood in order for growth to take place. It must be pointed out that failures should be kept to a minimum in the learning situation. Too many failures discourage the learner. A device that can be used to build confidence in the young pitcher is to take him out when he has pitched successfully for two or three innings. Look for an opportunity to remove him on a successful note. In this early learning stage avoid as much as possible removing a pitcher unless he has experienced some success. Your junior varsity and frosh coaches should cooperate in this confidence-building plan. The learning experience must be sprinkled with small successes.

Motivational devices

Using motivational devices is a skill that must be developed. Each pitcher has different needs and desires and the devices used must meet these needs. You will have to know your pitchers well and suit the motivation to the individual. A boy of little means might be shown how becoming a successful pitcher can afford him economic stability or enable him to get a college education. A rich boy who has everything can get great satisfaction from being on his own on the mound against great odds and succeeding without the aid of his money. The pitcher who is shy in social situations and desires to have more friends and be more popular will find that by attaining success in pitching he will belong to the group. The success coaches achieve in motivating is in direct proportion to how closely they fit the device to the individual. The pitcher who is well motivated will work on his own and will leave no stone unturned in his striving toward becoming successful.

Making a list of the possible motivating ideas that will fit a particular pitcher often helps the coach to understand the player better and to help him to realize his maximum potential. It is the coach's job to make the beginning pitcher's experience a rewarding one and to always keep his interest alive as he strives toward perfection. Imagination helps, but sincerity is most important in motivating young boys.

TIPS ON INSTRUCTIONAL TECHNIQUES

Much of the coach's time is spent in correcting errors, making suggestions for change, and reassuring the pitcher that what he is doing is sound. This is not a responsibility to be taken lightly. A haphazard unsubstantiated correction could well ruin a young pitcher's career. How can we guard against doing this? Coaches must have a thorough knowledge of pitching skills and must be aware of common faults and ways of correcting them. Throughout this book we will present the skills, bearing in mind the possible faults involved and how they can be corrected. When you have a good grasp of this knowledge the work has just begun. You still have to look at the pitcher, figure out what he is doing wrong and prescribe the remedy. This is not a cut-and-dried process and coaches will make mistakes, but the fear of making mistakes should not influence them to become a "that's-all-right, you're-ok" type of pitching coach. To keep errors to a minimum the approach to the solution of the problem must be well planned and as scientific as possible. We have organized the procedure under three general headings which should be followed carefully: (1) observation, (2) diagnosis, and (3) suggested remedy.

Observation

One of the major skills for the coach to develop is his ability to observe intelligently. It is true the coach may have certain cues for which he has learned to watch, but he must continuously check to make sure that he is really seeing what he thinks he is seeing. Often coaches see only what they want to see. You must be able to ferret out the important from the unimportant. Observation is not synonymous with looking or watching. Observation is a scientific process.

Let us look at some guidelines to careful pitching observation:

1. Observe with an open mind, ready to discover anything.
2. Observe the pitcher from many different angles.
3. Observe the pitcher when he is not aware of being observed.
4. Observe the end-result and work backward to the possible cause.
5. Observe the pitcher, bearing in mind his individual characteristics and idiosyncrasies. (No two pitchers are alike.)
6. Do not put a time limit on your observation. You may not see the flaw today but may catch it tomorrow.
7. Observe for a purpose. Focus your attention on the specific problem at hand.

Diagnosis

After careful observation, weigh what has been observed. Has enough been observed to make a diagnosis? Do not guess!! If it is not clear start the observation over again.

When the problem is narrowed down to two or three possible solutions, try them. Do this first in your mind and then, if need be, actually with the pitcher. But remember, too much experimentation with the pitcher will tend to confuse him. Bring into play your experience with similar problems in the past. What did you observe in these situations and what was their solution? You should keep a record of such problems. The diagnosis must grow out of what has *actually* been observed—not what you think the diagnosis should be. You might even call upon fellow experts and get their reactions to the diagnosis. Remember, however, in the end, the responsibility is yours.

Suggested remedy

We have observed carefully, used our knowledge of the skill, brought into play past experiences, experimented, and are now at the point of suggesting a remedy. As far as the pitcher is concerned the remedy you suggest is *it!* When the remedy is tried the process begins all over. Observe, diagnose, and check to see if you are getting the desired results. The suggested remedy after using the proposed method should have a 99% chance of being the right one. You cannot afford very many wrong guesses, so do not guess at all.

The case of the hanging curve

To further clarify the process let us look hypothetically at a very common problem. The pitcher's curve ball is not breaking sharply but is hanging up, where it is being hit hard. From knowledge about the curve ball it is known that this may be caused by any one or more of numerous faults: (1) not pulling down on the ball enough, (2) letting go of the ball too soon, (3) poor wrist action, (4) gripping the ball too tight, (5) gripping the ball too far back in the palm, (6) not getting on top of the pitch, or (7) improper rotation. The pitcher is observed carefully with the coach watching for these cues and looking out for other possible flaws. Observing from behind the pitcher it is ascertained that the rotation is adequate. The grip is checked and it is all right. Standing behind the plate it is observed that the pitcher is not getting on top of the pitch, it looks like he might be letting it go too soon. The pitcher claims he is making an effort to get on top but this does not seem to help. From the side, it is observed that the pitcher is taking a very long stride. Remembering from past experience that this can cause a pitcher to fail to get on top or pull down on the ball adequately, we mull it over in our mind and finally come to believe this is the solution, one that was not present in our original thinking. From careful observation and reflection the flaw was corrected. All cases may not be solved this easily but this general procedure will produce similar results, if followed conscientiously. Think, if you will, of the damage that might have been done to the pitcher's progress, if we should have let the matter ride or told him his fingers were too stubby to throw the curve, or that he would have to throw it harder to make it break. The responsibility to be a competent coach is a great one!

How does the pitcher learn?

To be a good pitching instructor, the coach must understand the different ways a pitcher learns. He must then make use of this information to efficiently instruct his pitchers. With this in mind, let us note some of the ways in which a pitcher might learn.

The pitcher might learn by observation, or *visual learning*. The coach's main tool of instruction under this heading is demonstration. He must point out certain cues (guides to action) involved in the pitching process. Movies can also be used as visual aids to instruction.

The pitcher sometimes learns through *verbal instruction*. Many coaches rely too heavily upon this means. The coaches' lament, "It goes in one ear and out the other" is oftentimes due to poor presentation on the part of the coach. Don't monopolize the instruction with long, wordy lectures.

The pitcher may also learn through *mechanical means.* By mechanical means, we refer to actually moving the pitcher's arm through a series of action. For example, the coach might hold the pitcher's elbow up, rather than demonstrate it or tell the pitcher to do it.

Some pitchers learn from *abstractions.* These abstractions could fall under several of the above categories. The example that is used in the chapter on the curve ball about throwing the curve around the barrel is an abstract way of learning. Generally the more intelligent pitcher can handle this type learning more easily than the less intelligent one.

The kinesthetic or "feel" type of learning is one of the most important. This type resembles the learning of the swimmer who does the frog kick even though he cannot see his legs doing it. He feels it. All pitchers must eventually "feel" their pitching. Some have a better kinesthetic sense than others. Pitchers of less than average intelligence often learn solely by this means.

The best way to instruct the pitcher

When you fully understand each pitcher and understand the different ways that individuals learn you are in a good position to effectively instruct your pitchers. A direct answer to the question of what is the best way to instruct the pitcher would have to be the method that gets the idea across the easiest at any given time. This is not as trite as it may sound. You will have to use your imagination and ingenuity to discover what method or methods work best for each pitcher.

The suggested plan for beginning the instruction is to use the whole-to-part-to-whole method. In other words, the pitcher should practice his whole delivery and then break it into parts. When these parts are improved, he then incorporates them back into his complete delivery. Concentrate on one aspect at a time. By this constant process of taking the delivery apart, practicing it and putting it back together, perfection is gained.

When the pitcher is working on one segment of pitching such as, having his wrist turned in on the curve ball, he should think of this only. Concentration on this one segment is the secret. When he has mastered this skill and puts it back into the whole again, it should be a fluid part of the whole motion, not one that sticks out in his mind over the others. When one learns how to drive he may concentrate on letting the clutch out, but when he becomes a skilled driver it is smoothly incorporated into the whole pattern of driving.

Successful coaches use imaginative devices in their instruction. These may be word-pictures, illustrative gimmicks, or other meaningful cues. The success of these devices is in direct proportion to how closely they are connected with the basic experiences of the pitcher. It would do no good to tell a boy who had never been out of Los Angeles to throw the ball as he would a snowball. This illustration would have meaning, however, to the boy raised in the midwest. Any device may be used to get the point across. Throughout this book we shall try to present many of these aids that have proved successful.

Repetition plays an important role in the instruction of pitching. But to be of value must be accompanied by reasoning and thought. In practice, the pitcher should get in the habit of throwing a pitch, analyzing its effectiveness, and then making improvements and corrections. We want him to be able to coach himself. Sneak up behind the pitcher when he is practicing, stop him, and ask him to analyze his last pitch. Why did it hang? Why did it break so well? Why was it thrown outside? He should learn to ask himself these questions. Twenty minutes of

this type practice is better than eight hours of meaningless repetition. The pitcher should be trained to paint a mental picture
of what he wants to do before delivering the pitch. He should
feel the action to be attempted ahead of time. The catcher calls
for a curve and immediately the pitcher should try to feel how
the pitch should be thrown. If he is *concentrating* on this he will
have no time to worry about failure. It is surprising how quickly
this skill can be developed through proper practice. This skill
of feeling a pitch prior to delivering may well be the most important single element to be developed.

The pitcher should not become discouraged with minor flaws
in his delivery and a coach should not dwell too much on these
minor imperfections. Many of them will iron themselves out
without being pointed out every time the pitcher practices.
Coaches who begin practice by telling the pitcher to remember
to "claw" the fast ball, follow through with the palm facing up,
keep the eyes on the target, get the hips into the pitch, and
watch the placement of the front foot, are impeding the learning! Do not try to teach too much, too fast. The drive toward
becoming a successful pitcher must be reinforced constantly
with success, to keep the drive alive. The pitcher will experience
many disappointments along the way; remind him of the pleas-
ures, rewards, and satisfactions that are to be derived through
becoming a successful pitcher.

Proper atmosphere for learning—beginners

For beginners to experience the greatest amount of learning,
the atmosphere should be free of tension. You should help them
to feel as relaxed as possible during the learning period. The
acquisition of skills is hard enough without the pitcher being
tense and nervous during the process. The learning pitcher
should not be distracted by pressures to win or succeed in a
hurry. The beginning pitcher is there to learn new skills, he is

not yet ready for the major battle. We *are* interested in winning but this emphasis comes later. Let your pitcher acquire the skills in a relaxed atmosphere. The instructional sessions should be short and should always end with some success.

Proper atmosphere for learning—advanced pitchers

The pace is now stepped up considerably. The pitchers have a good foundation of basic skills and are ready to enter the battle. These pitchers must learn to pitch under all types of pressure.

Our basic principle is to have the practice resemble as close as possible the game situation. It does not make sense to practice all week under no type of stress and then on Friday expect the pitcher to react properly in front of a large crowd with tension riding on every pitch. He must be prepared for this. The practice should be arranged with this in mind.

It is recommended that the "live stopper" drill on page 201, the "pressure drills" on page 203, and the "game situation" drill on page 202 be used in aiding the pitcher to cope with the pressures of the actual game. The pitcher should never become careless in practice. He should always be trying to test his pitches under pressure. The pitcher ought to constantly be making up imaginative situations in his mind to see if he can pitch his way out of them. If he is going to pitch twenty minutes, the last ten minutes should be under some type of assimilated pressure. He can simulate this pressure by going right down the opposing line-up. If he is not familiar with the opposing team, he can imagine pitching to his own line-up and pitch to each batter, setting them up and pitching to spots as he would in the actual game. This will get the pitcher physically and mentally in tune for the game.

The pitcher should also experience in practice, what it is like to pitch when tired. Pitching in the ninth inning is much different from pitching in the early innings when he is fresh. Many pitchers always throw in practice when they are fresh; no wonder they do not know how to react when they become shaky in the late innings.

There is a time, of course, when the advanced pitcher will be working on correcting a fault or striving to learn something new. When this is the case, the atmosphere should be the same as suggested for the beginner. Be sure you do not put a young pitcher under fire until he is ready, or his confidence will be badly shaken.

We want to teach our pitchers that choking stems only from the fear of the unknown. Our pitchers will not choke in difficult situations if they have met the situation before and know how to handle it. It is the coach's duty to prepare his pitchers to come through in these situations by having them meet these tight spots time and time again under every possible circumstance. Through efficient practices, many of these pressure situations can be met and conquered before anybody begins yelling choke on Friday. We tell our pitchers the story of the prowler who crawled in the bedroom window. If you are lying in bed watching him crawl in the window you are undoubtedly scared. There are two alternatives, you can lie there and say to yourself you are not afraid and let him hit you over the head, or you can admit you are afraid and figure a way to hit him first. How many pitchers have you seen get the bases loaded in a tight situation, look around like nothing is bothering them and then proceed to "walk the ball park" until help arrives? This type pitcher is so busy trying to act like he is not afraid that he does not meet the situation. We want our pitchers to admit they are in a tight spot and then do something positive about coming out on top.

Our method of gradually getting the pitcher ready for the battle can be paralleled to getting a person used to ice cold water by gradually placing him in cooler water until reaching the desired level. Be sure he has a reasonable chance of success before putting him in the situation. It may be a slow process but in the end we feel we will not only have a sounder pitcher but a sounder man.

The coach's responsibility to his pitchers

It has been established that the responsibility to be a competent coach is a great one. It is his duty to have the latest information on pitching instruction. This information can be obtained in many different ways.

Attendance at clinics is one of the best ways to pick up new ideas. Experts are usually called in to tell the group about their methods of success. This is oftentimes followed by a valuable question and answer period. It is suggested that the pitchers be allowed to attend the clinic, if for no other reason than to see how hard the coaches are working to become better instructors. If there are no clinics in your locality, organize one. Invite proven coaches to present their ideas and you will find that the clinic will be of tremendous benefit to all involved.

By reading the latest literature and the many fine articles in the various coaching journals much information can be picked up.

The pitching coach who wants to be a success must not be afraid to ask questions. We have found that seeking out authorities on pitching and plying them with questions has been of tremendous help to us. We also call our former pitchers back who have gone on to professional baseball and question them as to new methods and new ideas that they may have learned. Some coaches hesitate to ask questions as they feel it is admitting they do not know. We *must* admit we do not know everything, or growth cannot possibly take place.

As the coach of young pitchers, you are also responsible for a high caliber of moral leadership. You must be conscious of the great influence you have upon your pitchers. The young pitcher will probably follow the advice of his coach more than any other single leader in his life. He respects and admires his coach and looks to him for leadership in *life* as well as in *pitching.* You have ample opportunity to associate the valuable lessons learned through pitching to the everyday problems of the young pitcher.

By being a good example you can help your pitchers to become fine citizens. You should help your pitchers plan for the future and counsel them when the opportunity arises. You are in a good position to direct your players' excess energies into proper channels. The joys of coaching are winning, developing outstanding performers, and helping to develop young boys into outstanding men.

The push-button principle

The push-button principle is the ultimate goal we are trying to have our pitchers attain. It is the ability, for example, to be able to push a button for the curve ball, low and outside, and to deliver it. We realize that this ideal is not completely attainable, but the closer the pitcher gets to this goal, the greater will be his performance and success.

Our over-all pitching philosophy is based on this principle. When the pitchers are learning their basic skills, they are perfecting their ability to better answer the call of these push-buttons.

To illustrate our push-button concept, let us assume the batter is a fast ball hitter; there are no men on, no score, and it is early in the game. The pitcher wants to get the first pitch in there so he can get out in front and work on the batter. He mentally pushes the button for the "get-it-in-there curve." The batter takes it for a strike. He then throws a fast ball, high and inside, for a ball. The "get-it-in-there curve" is next for strike two and is followed by a poor curve, low and inside, a wasted pitch for ball two. On the next pitch the button is pushed for the "extra curve" which the batter has not seen, and so he goes down swinging. The pitcher showed the batter three average curves and then drove him back with a fast ball, before getting him with the extra curve. Throughout this process, we want the pitcher to think he was just pushing buttons.

This idea is a great mental aid. It allows the boy to concentrate and to think about the job at hand, and more important, it keeps him from thinking about failing. The pitcher should end up thinking about what has to be done, not whether he can do it. The buttons will take care of that.

◆ The Pitcher's Physical Conditioning

three

Physical conditioning must not be overlooked in planning for the pitcher's development. Your pitcher may have good stuff and pin-point control but if he is not in good physical condition he will be of little value to your team. He will tire in the late innings and will hurt you in the important games during the latter part of the season. The push-button principle relies upon the pitcher's delicate control of his mental and physical processes. If the pitcher's legs are shaky, if he is winded, or if his arm is tired, he is not in full command of his processes.

In the past, many boys were considered poor pitching prospects because they were too weak. Today there is no excuse for being weak. The six-foot two inch, one hundred fifty pounder no longer need take a back seat because he is weak. Through a well supervised strength development program he can build himself into a powerful pitcher. We have not found the secret for making a boy taller but we can certainly help a boy become stronger.

The pitcher should not only keep his body in top physical condition but he must continuously strive to build and to strengthen his equipment. The pitcher must not be content with adding strength through age, he must be willing to work, to overload his body in order to add strength. It is your duty as coach to keep your pitchers at their maximum physical efficiency and also to aid them in developing additional strength. For an individual to keep physically fit and to add strength, he must push himself beyond the point where it begins to hurt. Very few people have the willpower to push themselves this hard. You, as coach, will have to be the pusher. As in any other activity in which you are trying to get the optimum out of an individual, best results are obtained when the subject is well motivated and the means used to accomplish the desired goals are efficient. In this chapter we shall present ways in which strength can be developed in the off-season, showing how fitness can be maintained in the off-season, how the pre-season conditioning program can best be handled and how to maintain the pitcher's physical condition throughout the regular season.

OFF-SEASON STRENGTH DEVELOPMENT

To develop strength, the part being developed has to be overloaded. To overload is to force the part to make a maximum effort to overcome a resistance (to go beyond what can be done easily). When more resistance is added, more muscle fibers have to be brought into play to overcome the resistance, thus the growth in strength. It is important in any strength-building program to continuously increase the amount of resistance. To continue working under the same amount of resistance results in little growth in strength.

The program of strength development involves use of weights, apparatus, calisthenics, or isometric training. A sound program might very well include all of these items.

The use of weights and apparatus

For many years the use of weights for pitchers was frowned upon. It was felt that the pitchers would become muscle-bound and tight and would lose the whiplike action that pitchers need. In the past ten years authorities have changed their views. Many successful pitchers owe a great amount of their success to well planned weight lifting programs. The program must be well supervised as most of the criticism in the past has been aimed at the "T-shirt-filler" type lifting that can be so harmful to pitchers. Throughout the program the specific purpose for which the strengthening is being done must be borne in mind— that of improving the performance of the pitcher. The exercises should not be done to add bulk but to increase explosive power —a combination of speed and strength.

The exercises should be done through a full range of movement. That is to say, the exercises should as closely as possible resemble the movements involved in the actual pitching motion. As an example of this principle, the two-hand press that is a part of every weight lifting system should be done with a strong, quick, thrusting action rather than a slow, sluggish movement.

Stretching

The most important principle of the entire weight training program for pitchers is the stretching rule. The pitcher must stretch after each exercise period to maintain his body flexibility. Without stretching, the weight program can do serious damage. The best method of stretching is to hang limply from a high bar. This hanging action stretches the muscles and helps maintain flexibility. If no bar is available the pitcher may hang from a door or similar object. Under no circumstances should you allow the pitcher to lift weights without stretching afterwards. Calisthenics for the purpose of stretching should be done each day.

Apparatus such as wall pulleys, bars, and general gym equipment can be used, keeping in mind the same principles that are involved in the weight program. Coaches must closely supervise the weight programs of their pitchers or serious damage may result. It is better to have no weight program at all than to have an unsupervised one.

In setting up the weight program it is wise to begin with the development of the major muscle groups first and then work on specific muscles. There are hundreds of exercises that may be used, but we feel that by limiting the program to no more than ten exercises the pitcher can be developed effectively. Hooks presented a group of exercises many of which we have incorporated into our strength building program.[1] Our recommended weight program for pitchers is presented below. The recommended weight to be used is what we have found to be average for beginners, although it will vary according to individual strength. The weight should be increased five pounds when the lifter can execute ten repetitions with the heaviest weight.

1. Dumbbell Arm-Circle. Loosening up exercise. Full arm circles with light dumbbells and then full circles with the wrists.
2. Hip Swing. The bar bell is placed across the small of the back in the crook of the elbows, the pitcher takes his stride and rotates his hips as in pitching. Thirty repetitions. (Begin with forty-five pounds.)
3. Wrist Roller. The pitcher holds a bar in his hands which has a rope hanging from it attached to a weight. The pitcher rolls the weight up by rolling the bar in his hands.
4. Wrist Rotator. The pitcher holds a dumbbell, loaded at one end in his hand and rotates it from side to side using his wrist only.
5. Two-Hand Press. Thrust at top. Ten repetitions with forty-five pounds, eight with fifty pounds, and six with fifty-five pounds.
6. Shoulder Shrugs. Twenty repetitions with fifty-five pounds. (Lifter holds bar bell at arms length *down* in front of him and raises it by shrugging shoulders toward his ears.)
7. Forward Press. The same as the throwing motion with quick thrust at the end. Ten repetitions with twenty pounds, eight with twenty-five pounds, and six with thirty pounds.
8. Two-Hand Curl. Ten repetitions with thirty-five pounds, eight with forty pounds, and six with forty-five pounds.
9. Squats. Two sets of ten repetitions with fifty-five pounds. Stay on the toes and execute in a quick jumping motion.

[1] G. E. Hooks, *Application of Weight Training To Athletics.* Englewood Cliffs, N. J., Prentice-Hall, Inc., 1962, pp. 123–134.

10. Wrist Curls. Sitting position, forearms resting on the thighs. Ten repetitions with twenty pounds, eight with twenty-five pounds, six with thirty pounds.

A supplemental exercise that is causing wide-spread attention among pitching coaches is the use of weighted balls in developing the specific pitching muscles. In this particular exercise the pitcher must be cautious to throw through a full range of motion so as not to damage the elbow.

The use of calisthenics

Calisthenics lack the efficiency of weights and apparatus as a strength developer. It takes too long to overload a muscle group through calisthenics. Calisthenics play an important part in maintaining body flexibility. An effective strength development program should include calisthenics to help balance the over-all development of the body. Calisthenics also have considerable value as a warmup activity for more strenuous exercises to follow. The stretching exercises should be done slowly past the point where it hurts. The recommended calisthenics program is presented below.

1. Wing Stretcher. Stand erect, raise elbows to shoulder height, fists clenched, palms down in front of chest. Thrust elbow backward vigorously and return.
2. Alternate Toe Toucher. Feet apart, hands outstretched, alternate opposite hand to opposite toe.
3. Eight Count Trunk Rotation. Feet apart, hands on hips, rotate trunk side, front, and back slowly.
4. Sit-Ups.
5. Finger-Tip Push-Ups.
6. Hurdler's Stretch. Sit on ground with legs in hurdlers' position, stretch to touch front toe.
7. Bicycle Peddling. On back, peddling legs, concentrating on knee action.
8. Opposite Leg to Opposite Hand Stretch. On back, arms outstretched; stretch the opposite leg to touch opposite hand.
9. Six-Inch Leg Raiser. On back, feet together; raise feet six inches off the ground separate, together, and down.

10. Wood Chopper. Feet apart, hands with fists clenched over head; bring arms down vigorously between legs as in chopping wood.

The use of isometric training

Isometric exercises have been receiving considerable attention. In executing an isometric exercise, the part of the body being exercised pushes or pulls against an object or another part of the body. During the movement the muscle does not decrease in length. An isometric exercise could parallel the two-hand press as in the following example: the arms push upward, as in the press, except against a *stable* bar rather than a barbell, using at least a two-thirds maximum effort. It is claimed that an exercise such as this, held for a period of six seconds, would result in maximum strength gains. The use of isometric training could prove to be a valuable time-saver. The weakness of these exercises seems to rest in their inability to build endurance, and flexibility.

WINTER FITNESS

While we are building strength we want to be certain that the pitchers are maintaining a level of pitching fitness. They should keep their arms in condition by throwing periodically during the week. You must avoid the danger of putting so much emphasis on strength building procedures that you forget about maintaining the boy's pitching skills.

The pitcher should be increasing his pitching skills in conjunction with his strength building program. It is important that he pitch frequently so that he will learn to adapt to his added strength.

Weight control

Before beginning the winter program you must determine which of your pitchers have a tendency toward overweight and which need to gain weight. Weight charts should be kept on the pitchers as a check for you and as an added stimulus to the boys. If the pitcher has a serious weight problem he should see a physician. Usually the physician will be willing to cooperate with you and the boy in recommending a diet and conferring with you on a proper training routine. The boy we are most often concerned with, however, is the one who tends to lie around and put on weight in the off-season, making it very difficult for him to get into playing shape when the season begins. Some pitchers of this type never do get into shape until it is too late. Coaches, by organizing a well-rounded winter program, can help avoid much of this trouble.

Recommended activities

To get the most out of the activity program it should be made interesting and competitive. Much running and vigorous exercise can be had through games and other activities.

The program should include all types of running: quick starts, distance running, wind-sprints, and base-running. Running the bases and wind-sprints should be timed and records kept to add interest. It is recommended that all the pitchers be able to run the mile in at least six minutes, before the season begins. It is up to the individual pitcher to get himself down to this time.

Badminton, handball, and two-man volleyball are good conditioning games for pitchers in the winter. These games should be as competitive as possible in order to get the most out of the pitchers. The major purpose of the running and games is to serve as a change of pace in the strength-building program and to maintain a minimum level of physical condition throughout the year.

The activity part of the winter program will usually be run two days a week. For simplicity, the activities have been divided into three major categories. In each activity period, at least one phase under each heading should be covered. Several different activities are presented to add variety to the program.

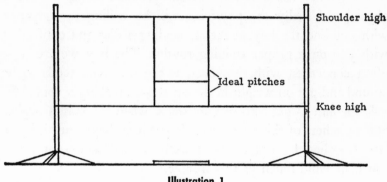

Shoulder high

Ideal pitches

Knee high

Illustration 1
String Target

1. Throwing
   a. Throwing through the strings for control.
   b. Working on the development of pitching technique.
   c. Stretching the arm by throwing easily with a full arm motion from a greater distance than sixty feet.
2. Movement Activity
   a. Pepper game (no more than three in a group).
   b. Pitcher's fielding drill (see drill number twenty page 204).
   c. Two-man volleyball, badminton, or handball.
3. Running Activity
   a. Sprints for time. (Record.)
   b. Run the bases for time. (Record.)
   c. Competitive relays.
   d. Mile run. (Under six minutes.)

Recommended winter program

We have covered all phases of the winter program. These included both strength development and the maintenance of pitching fitness. Under these categories, specific activities were recommended.

The proposed winter schedule is set up for a five-day program of approximately one hour duration. Monday, Wednesday, and

Friday will be spent specifically on strength development and Tuesdays and Thursdays on maintaining pitching fitness. The specific activities will be referred to by the numbers used in the preceding sections in the chapter. Coaches may vary the schedule to meet their individual needs; however, the ideas of alternating strength building with activities related to pitching is advised so that the development does not become one-sided. Below, a sample of two weeks of the winter program is presented:

The first week

Monday
1. Warmup Calisthenics 1, 2, 3, 6, 8, and 10.
2. Weight Lifting Exercises 1 through 10. (Use recommended repetitions, pages 54 and 55.)
3. Jog 440.

Tuesday
1. Calisthenics 1 through 10.
2. Throwing Exercise c.
3. Running Activity b.
4. Movement Activity a.

Wednesday
1. Warmup Calisthenics 1, 2, 3, 6, 8, and 10.
2. Weight Lifting Exercises 1 through 10. (Recommended repetitions.)
3. Jog 880.

Thursday
1. Calisthenics 1 through 10.
2. Throwing Exercise a.
3. Running Activity c.
4. Movement Activity b.

Friday
1. Warmup Calisthenics 1, 2, 4, 6, 8, and 10.
2. Weight Lifting Exercises 1 through 10. (Recommended repetitions.)
3. Jog 880.

The second week

Monday

1. Warmup Calisthenics 1, 2, 3, 6, 8, and 10.
2. Weight Lifting Exercises 1 through 10. (Recommended repetitions.)
3. Jog 440.

Tuesday

1. Calisthenics 1 through 10.
2. Throwing Exercise b.
3. Running Activity c.
4. Movement Activity c. (Pick one of the three.)

Wednesday

1. Warmup Calisthenics 1, 2, 4, 6, 8, and 10.
2. Weight Lifting Exercises 1 through 10. (Decrease weight ten pounds and lift for speed.)
3. Jog 880.

Thursday

1. Calisthenics 1 through 10.
2. Throwing Exercise b.
3. Running Activity d.
4. Movement Activity. (None. After running mile.)

Friday

1. Warmup Calisthenics 1, 2, 3, 6, 8, and 10.
2. Weight Lifting Exercises 1 through 10. (Increase the weight to maximum and lower repetitions.)
3. Jog 440.

By varying this program and using the recommended exercises, a well-rounded program can be maintained during the off-season, and by regrouping you can put the weekly emphasis where you feel it is most needed. It must be remembered that the program will vary according to the needs of the individual pitchers. For example, the overweight pitcher will need a different emphasis from that of the underweight pitcher.

PRE-SEASON CONDITIONING

The problems that coaches face in getting their pitchers in shape for the coming season are certainly made simpler when the winter program is a good one. Even with a good winter program, however, you will be receiving your pitchers in various stages of physical condition. The building phase is over, you must now tone up your pitcher's specific "equipment" and get him ready for battle. Coaches usually have approximately a month to do this before the first game.

Getting the legs and body in shape

It has often been said, "So go a pitcher's legs, so goes his arm." This is not an over-statement of the importance of the condition of the pitcher's legs. There is no easy way to get the legs in condition. The pitcher must run, run, run! This running can, however, be made as interesting as possible to get more out of the pitcher. You will have to remember that you are going to have to do a certain amount of forcing to get your pitchers into shape. You will have to be a task-master. Interjecting competition and variety into the running will make the task much easier.

Timed wind-sprints get more out of the pitcher than merely telling him to run ten. Running the bases for time also gives the pitcher incentive. The pick-up drill, the football pass drill, the fungo drill, the pitcher's fielding drill, acting as runners in game situations, and the ten yard sprint drill add variety to the running program. (See drill numbers twenty-five through thirty-three.) You can use these various drills to "spice" up your pre-season conditioning program.

Practice should be interspersed with running. The running should not necessarily be saved until last. Some warmup running can be done before practice, several of the drills may be used during practice, and the hard running can be done at the end of practice. At the end of this section several pre-season practices are presented as examples.

The peak of condition should be worked up to gradually. Coaches should not kill their pitchers the first day. Inform the pitchers how important conditioning of the legs is and show them where it fits into their over-all pitching excellence. A well motivated pitcher will get into top condition much sooner than the one who is not. Give him a reason for running!

Getting the body in shape certainly includes running, but added to these running activities must be stretching exercises to aid the pitcher in maintaining the flexibility he will need. Calisthenics and stretching from the bar are very important during the pre-season conditioning period. The stretching must be done slowly, avoiding jerkiness. By stretching slowly past the hurting point flexibility can be gained and injury avoided. The body should be warmed up properly before strenuous activity. Calisthenics (one through ten) are recommended to aid in warmup and stretching.

Getting the arm in shape

The pitcher should start getting his "major weapon," his arm, ready for battle gradually. The pitcher should begin by throwing medium fast balls for about ten minutes and gradually increase this time to twenty or thirty minutes after the first week. When he has reached the twenty minute phase he should take periodic one-day rest periods from pitching, and on those days run and field only. At the end of the first week he can begin spinning the curve. He must be cautioned to use the full arm motion so as not to strain the elbow or shoulder. The pitcher should gradually begin to put more on his fast ball and to spin the curve each day.

The pitcher should not throw batting practice until he has pitched for about ten days. More experienced ball players may be able to pitch batting practice sooner (professionals) as they are wise enough not to push themselves too far. The young pitcher in trying to impress may injure himself. Impress upon the pitcher that this pre-season period is for the purpose of getting into shape not for the purpose of making the team and arm trouble will be kept to a minimum.

When do I start bearing down is a question often asked by the young pitcher. There is no set answer for this. If the pitcher will steadily increase his conditioning and extend his arm a little further each day he will gradually approach 100% bearing down efficiency.

Pitching in pre-season intra-squad games should be handled in the same manner as the over-all pre-season conditioning program. The pitcher should gradually work up to the point where he can go the distance.

Proper care of the arm

You should educate the pitcher to know his own arm. The pitcher is the only one who can really take care of his arm. With proper guidance from you he can guard against arm miseries. Let us look at some of the guiding principles for the pitcher:

1. Do not let the arm cool off in a draft.
2. Always wear a wool sweat shirt (or with at least some percentage of wool).
3. Never be without a jacket.
4. Wear the jacket *after* pitching and *after* warming up, not during the actual pitching.
5. Start warming up ahead of time so that the arm has the proper time to get loose.
6. Gradually work up to maximum efficiency.
7. Report any arm trouble to the coach. (No matter how minor.)
8. Do not pitch with a sore arm.
9. After showering, dry carefully and wear a warm jacket home.
10. The pitcher must adjust his warmup period to the weather. (Shorter in warm weather—longer in cold weather.)

If it is a cold day and it is felt that the pitcher needs to protect his arm with more warmth an ointment may be applied. Rubdowns are sometimes beneficial but the person administering the rubdown must know what he is doing or it may be dangerous, or at best ineffective. The pitcher should not come to rely on ointments and rubdowns.

The whirlpool should never be used before a game, as it tends to sap the strength from the pitcher's arm. There are times following a pitching stint when the whirlpool and a carefully supervised rubdown can be an aid to removing arm stiffness.

In the early season, a stiff feeling in the arm is most common. Many times this stiffness can be worked out by getting the whole arm into the pitch. Stretching exercises and hanging from the bar are valuable at this time. If the pain is in the elbow or shoulder a competent trainer or physician should be consulted.

Pre-season practices

Below are presented samples of practice schedules for pitchers during the first three weeks of the season.

Typical Day During the First Week:

1. Ten minutes of calisthenics (Exercises 1, 2, 3, 4, 6, 7, 8, 9, and 10).
2. Jog 440.
3. Throw for ten minutes (after getting the arm loose.)
4. Pick-up drill 25.
5. Hit pepper. (No more than three in a group.)
6. Fungo drill.
7. Ten timed sixty-yard wind-sprints.

Typical Day During the Second Week:

During this week a day for resting the arm should be set aside in which the pitcher does not throw at all.)

1. Ten minutes of calisthenics. (Exercises 1, 2, 3, 4, 6, 7, 8, 9, and 10.)
2. Fifteen to twenty minutes throwing, putting a little more on the fast ball, after getting the arm loose.

3. Pick-up drill 40.
4. Run the bases for time. (Once.)
5. Hit pepper.
6. Football pass drill. Ten without missing.
7. Ten sixty-yard wind-sprints (run one, walk one) interspersed with twenty-yard sprint drill.

Typical Day During the Third Week:

The pitcher should throw only on Monday, Wednesday, and Friday this week. Emphasize running and fielding on Tuesday and Thursday.

1. Ten minutes of calisthenics. (Exercises 1, 2, 3, 4, 5, 7, 8, 9, and 10.)
2. Twenty minutes of throwing. (Include spinning the curve.)
3. Pitcher's fielding drill.
4. Fungo drill.
5. Hit pepper.
6. Pick-up drill 50.
7. Run the mile under six minutes.

KEEPING IN CONDITION DURING THE SEASON

Once the pitcher is in shape and taking his turn in the pitching rotation the conditioning program is more of a maintenance problem. The pitcher still must run and do calisthenics, but for a different purpose. He must keep himself in top physical condition to compete. He must not run so much that he leaves his ball game on the practice field nor should he become careless in his training and thus fall out of condition. The amount of running he should do will depend on his position in the team's pitching rotation and his over-all physical characteristics.

Pitching rotation

To help coaches plan their programs during the season we include examples of several types of rotation plans. It is felt that at least one of these hypothetical samples will suit each coach's individual need.

The Once-a-Week Pitcher

In many school situations the pitcher is called upon to take his turn just once a week. On the high school level this is recommended. You will have to make sure that the pitcher remains sharp during the lay-off. There is some controversy whether a pitcher should touch a ball the day after he pitches. We feel that he should throw just enough to get the kinks out.

To aid in preparing your weekly pitching plan for the once-a-week pitcher, two schedules are included. From these you can adopt a plan to fit your individual situation. We will suppose that the pitcher is going to pitch on Tuesdays. (The plan will work for any day.) The plans are classified under two headings, the pitcher with good control and the pitcher with poor control. We feel the pitcher with poor control needs more pitching during the week than the pitcher with good control. The coach must know his pitcher and vary the plan accordingly.

The Pitcher with Good Control:

1. Tuesday. Pitch the ball game.
2. Wednesday. Take the kinks out. (Light throwing, pepper, and run.)
3. Thursday. Throw fifteen or twenty minutes working on pitches and run.
4. Friday. Throw a round of batting practice, stopper drill, game situation drill, or mental drill. One of these choices only.
5. Saturday. Rest.
6. Sunday. Throw fifteen or twenty minutes and run.
7. Monday. Rest.
8. Tuesday. Pitch the game.

The Pitcher with Poor Control:

1. Tuesday. Pitch the ball game.
2. Wednesday. Take the kinks out. (Light throwing, pepper, and run.)

3. Thursday. Throw fifteen or twenty minutes through strings.
4. Friday. Throw twenty minutes' game situation drill.
5. Saturday. Rest.
6. Sunday. Throw twenty minutes through the strings.
7. Monday. Loosen up and check pitches for control.
8. Tuesday. Pitch the game.

The Twice-a-Week Pitcher

It is not recommended that a pitcher start twice a week. In some instances when you only have one good pitcher you may want to have him start one game and be ready for relief in the other. This pitcher gets little actual pitching practice and has very little time to develop anything new, once the season starts. It is important that you be aware of this as he must be equipped for battle when the season starts. There will not be time to add to his wares as the season progresses. If he starts on Tuesday he should loosen up on Wednesday, rest on Thursday and be ready to go Friday.

The relief pitcher

It is difficult to set up an exact plan for the relief pitcher. He may be called in to relieve in the first inning and finish the game, he may only pitch to one batter, or he may not pitch at all. He must have a strong arm to begin with and thrive on work. He cannot work on development once the season begins as he has to have his arm rested and ready to go on Tuesday and Friday. You cannot afford to over-work him and you cannot afford to let him lose his sharpness. He should get as much work in as possible following a game in which he did not pitch much. He must then rest and be ready for the next game. He should spend much of his time running and when possible work in the stopper drill.

No matter what the pitching rotation the pitcher should run and do his calisthenics each day. As pitchers gain experience they learn to know themselves better. They are becoming pros. If they feel they are more effective when they loosen up the day before pitching, allow them to do so. If they feel better when they do not throw the day after pitching let them rest.

The day of the game routine

The pitcher should get sufficient sleep the night before he pitches and should eat a light lunch at least three hours before game time. The food should be easy to digest and not highly seasoned.

The coach should go over the game plans the night before or early in the day so that this will not have to be done hurriedly before the game. The pitcher should get to the dressing room early enough so that he will not have to hurry to dress. Fifteen minutes before he is going to warm up he should go out to the field and sit in the dugout. He can check the other teams' hitters and think how he is going to pitch to them.

The length of time it takes to warm up varies with each pitcher. As a general rule heavy muscled pitchers take longer to warm up than thin muscled pitchers. The age of the pitcher and the weather also have much to do with how long it takes a pitcher to get loose. Again, the pitcher will have to know himself. He should do some light stretching exercises before warming up. Remember, many a pitcher is knocked out of the box because he is still warming up while facing the first four batters.

The pre-game warmup procedure

The pitcher should warm up in the same direction as he is going to pitch in the game. The mound should be similar to the actual game mound. The warmup period should be started gradually. He should throw easily at first using his full arm motion, throwing medium fast balls for about five minutes and working on his control. The pitcher should now spin some curve balls until his arm is completely loose. He can then bear down more on his fast ball and curve and work on his change-up. He should pitch from the stretch position as well as from the wind-up position. When his arm feels good and he is throwing his pitches at game speed he should set up two or three imaginary hitters and pitch to them like he would in the game. This helps to do away with pre-game jitters and lets him know when he is ready. The average warmup period for a pitcher is from fifteen to twenty minutes. He should finish his warmups five minutes before game time, put on his jacket, and sit down in the dugout, ready to go. You must refrain from teaching the pitcher how to pitch during his warmups. If he does not know it by now he is not going to know it.

The pitcher during the game

The pitcher should try to conserve his energy as much as possible during the game. He should walk briskly to and from the mound, but should not run. He should not stalk aimlessly around the mound performing needless, energy-consuming actions. The catcher can help him by throwing the ball back to him accurately. Between innings the pitcher should relax as much as possible and stay off his feet. If he has run the bases or had a short inning in which to rest, his teammates should take this into consideration and give him time to rest.

The pitcher's warmup tosses between innings should be meaningful. He should not just go out to the mound and lob the ball. If he is having trouble with a certain pitch he should work on it. He should pitch as if he were facing the first batter. He should not go out to the mound as if on his last legs, for this would make him feel more tired than he really is and may wake up the hitters. The pitcher should walk to the mound briskly as if looking forward to the inning. The adage, "You are only as old as you feel," might be compared with the pitching slogan, "You are only as tired as you act."

After the game

The pitcher should put on his jacket, quickly acknowledge his congratulations or condolences and get into a hot shower. He should not hang around outside and let his arm cool off. After thoroughly drying he should put on a warm shirt and jacket before going outside. (We have our pitchers come to the office and pick up their charts and discuss the game briefly before going home. The condition of his arm is ascertained at this time. This meeting is also for the purpose of letting him cool off gradually, both mentally and physically. It is a quiet moment in which the pitcher learns something—whether he won or lost.) The coach can use this period to stimulate the pitcher toward the next *win!*

◆ Form and Delivery

four

Proper form and delivery in pitching are different for each individual. Although there are certain common and basic techniques that should be followed by all successful pitchers, for each one there is still a best way to pitch. The coach must help the pitcher determine which way is best for him, so that the pitcher reaches maximum efficiency through the building of sound form and delivery.

In this chapter the basic techniques of form and delivery for the successful pitcher will be discussed. Methods of teaching these techniques and simplified ways of helping the pitchers acquire them are also presented.

DETERMINING PROPER ARM ANGLE

The angle of delivery may range from directly over-hand to under-hand. Each pitcher must find the angle at which he functions most effectively and then stick with it. Every pitch should be thrown from the same angle so that the pitcher will not tip his pitches. If he throws his fast ball side-arm and his curve ball over-hand it is obvious that the batter will know what is coming. Also, for reasons of control (discussed in chapter eight) each pitch should be thrown from the same arm angle.

The over-hand or three-quarter delivery

This type of delivery is the most used because it is the most natural delivery for the majority of pitchers. The fast ball will usually hop and the pitcher can also throw a good down-breaking curve from this same position. Further, the over-hand or three-

71

quarter pitch is usually easier to control. Somewhere between directly over-hand and three-quarters (between twelve o'clock and two o'clock) is the best natural angle of delivery.

The side-arm delivery

Occasionally you will run across the pitcher whose natural delivery is side-arm. He has nothing over-hand but is quite effective throwing side-arm. Still, there are several disadvantages to the side-arm delivery. It is virtually impossible to perfect a down-breaking curve from the side-arm angle. The curve is usually flat and ineffective. If the pitcher brings the arm angle up to throw the curve he will be tipping his pitch. However, if he is right handed, his fast ball will usually be effective against right hand hitters (and vice versa) although it may lose its effectiveness against left handed hitters because they are not intimidated by the delivery. Without the down-breaking curve the side-arm pitcher loses some of his effectiveness against opposite side hitters, as the flat curve will be breaking into the hitters power. Further the side-arm pitcher will usually experience more control problems because he has to contend with the horizontal plane of the strike zone as well as the vertical plane. (See chapter eight.) The side-armer may compensate by throwing a sinker (see chapter seven) but this is sometimes difficult for the young pitcher. Additionally the side-arm delivery is often harder on the arm than the over-hand or three-quarter delivery.

Determining which delivery is best for each pitcher

From the foregoing, it can be seen that the over-hand or three-quarter delivery holds decided advantages over the side-arm delivery. The young pitcher, however, should not be forced into a specific type delivery.

The best way to determine which arm angle is the most natural for the pitcher is to observe him when he is playing regular catch, or to hit him ground balls and have him throw to first base, observing his most natural throwing angle.

If the boy is set in his ways it is best to let him throw from the angle that is most comfortable for him. If he is a beginning pitcher it is sometimes possible to alter the pitching angle in order to improve his effectiveness.

If the boy is tall and lean and throws with a loose buggy-whip side-arm motion it may be wise to allow him to remain side-arm. There have been several of these types who have become effective major league pitchers.

The pitcher will have to arrive at the decision himself but you can have a lot to do with steering him in the proper direction. The exact angle, whether it be seventy-five degrees, sixty degrees, etc., is arrived at through trial and error. Once the most efficient arm angle for the individual is determined, he should throw every pitch from this exact angle. (It is noted that certain major league pitchers are able to vary their arm angle from time to time, but this is not recommended for the young pitcher.)

PRELIMINARY ACTIONS

The wind-up position

When receiving the sign with no men on base the front foot should be in contact with the rubber with the front spikes extending over the front of the rubber. To facilitate a shorter pivot the toes of the front foot are pointed at a slight angle toward third base for right handers and toward first base for left handers. (Illustration number 2.)

Reasons for the wind-up. There are five basic reasons for the wind-up: (1) It tends to loosen the pitcher's body and relieve tension, allowing his body to function to the maximum in delivering the pitch. (2) In every athletic skill there is a preliminary movement to get the action started. In hitting it may be

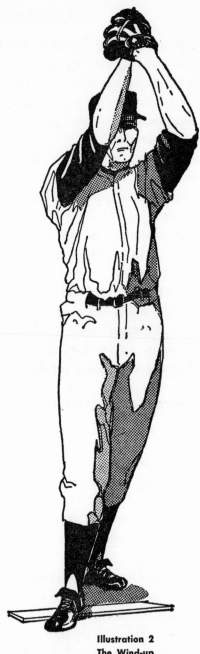

Illustration 2
The Wind-up
74

a slight movement or hitch of the hands; in golf it is the preliminary movement of the hands and body forward and then back into the swing; in pitching it is the wind-up. (3) The wind-up some times confuses the batter and upsets his timing. (4) It helps the pitcher's rhythm of delivery. (5) It assists the pitcher in hiding the ball with his body and its movements.

Use of the single, double, and triple pump

If the pitcher uses the same rhythm on every pitch, the batter will soon begin hitting off his rhythm, i.e., the batter will base his hitting rhythm on the constant rhythm of the pitcher. The pitcher must somehow upset the batter's rhythm. To do this he should vary his pumps, pumping once, twice, and sometimes three times. He can also vary the speed of one pump. The pitcher should vary the time intervals between pitches.

The "no-wind-up" pitcher

In past years several major league pitchers have been successful using no wind-up at all. There are many reasons for the no-wind-up approach. It may be used to break up the rhythm as explained previously. Some pitchers who have control difficulties find that the no-wind-up technique aids their control because it simplifies the movements they have to coordinate in order to deliver the ball with maximum efficiency. Some pitchers lose some of their stuff during the wind-up. Their coordination is such that the wind-up impedes their efficiency rather than increases it. An example of this would be the pitcher who does not get over the top and out in front to release the ball at the most advantageous point because his wind-up has thrown his coordination off. By using no wind-up the pitcher's motion is simplified and he may be able to get "more" behind the pitch. It also aids pitchers who otherwise have difficulty hiding the ball in the regular wind-up. Taking the wind-up away from some pitchers would completely ruin their pitching coordination, while in others it helps immeasurably. This is an individual matter that you and the boy will have to solve. It is certainly something worth considering if your pitcher's coordination seems to be off and he does not seem to be getting the most out of his delivery.

Hiding the ball

While taking the sign the ball should be hidden behind the leg or in the small of the back. (Illustration 3.) When the pitcher starts his wind-up the ball should be hidden in the glove with the ball well up into the web of the glove so that the pitching hand is hidden by the glove. (Illustration 2.) As the pitcher makes his pivot the ball is hidden behind the glove, and then his body so that the batter does not see it until it is coming toward him.

Tipping pitches

Many high school pitchers tip their pitches and even some pitchers in professional baseball are guilty of some tell-tale idiosyncrasy that gives their pitches away. Many games can be won by alert coaches who pick up the pitches of the opposing pitcher. Coaches that know the other team is picking up their pitches and do not know what to do about it are letting their pitchers down. To aid you in guarding against the danger of your pitcher tipping his pitches let us look at a list of the ways pitchers might tip their pitches.

1. Changing arm angles on different pitches.
2. Pumping higher on one type pitch than on another.
3. Raising the leg higher on one type pitch than on another.
4. Turning the wrist more on one pitch than another as the pitching hand goes up in the glove.
5. Turning the wrist in (usually on the curve) as the pitching hand comes by the side of the pitcher in the back swing.
6. Spreading the fingers on certain type pitches and not on others.

Illustration 3
Taking the Sign

77

7. Showing more white on certain pitches.
8. Turning the glove differently when delivering certain pitches.

These are some of the more obvious give-aways of which pitchers may be guilty. You will have to study each pitcher closely to discover if he is tipping his pitches. Sometimes even the change in facial expressions is a give-away.

To avoid tipping his pitches the pitcher should strive to throw every pitch in the same manner. He should hide the ball well up in the web of his glove. If he knows the other team is picking up his pitches and he discovers how, he can quickly discourage them from guessing by tipping the curve purposely and throwing the fast ball. The pitcher should guard against trying to change his pitch in the middle of his delivery.

The set position

The set position is used when there is a runner on base. The right handed pitcher is facing the third base line and the left handed pitcher is facing first base. The back foot is up against the front of the rubber and parallel to it. The feet are spread comfortably with the weight equally distributed on each foot. The front shoulder should be in a direct line with the plate. If the pitcher has his front shoulder toward first base the runner will get the jump when he turns it back toward the plate to pitch. Just as the pitcher has to be careful to avoid tell-tale tip-offs on his pitches he also has to be careful not to tip-off his move to first; his actions must be the same when he is going home as when he is *going to first*. The right handed pitcher should have his head in such a position that he can see the runner on first out of the corner of his eye. He should not let the runner get a walking start. If he catches the runner leaning he should throw over to first.

The pitcher must develop his techniques from the stretch position so that he does not have an exaggerated leg kick which gives the runner a jump. He must remember to pause at least one second after coming to the set position before throwing to the plate. The pitcher should get the same push off the rubber in the stretch as he does in the wind-up. The techniques for the good delivery are the same from the set position as they are from the wind-up with the possible exceptions of cutting down the leg kick and speeding up the process slightly.

Many young pitchers become ineffective with men on base. They worry so much about the runners that their pitching suffers. The pitcher must continually practice from the set position and perfect his delivery so that he gets just as much on the ball from this position as he does from his wind-up. One of the great advantages of a good base runner is that oftentimes he worries the pitcher so much that the pitcher loses his effectiveness. The pitcher must not alter his form so much, in order to perfect his move, that he no longer can get the man at the plate out. The actual pick-off moves and methods of holding the runner on will be presented in chapter ten.

COILING ACTION

Throughout the remainder of the chapter the descriptions of the pitching motion will be for the right handed pitcher. For the left handed pitcher the directions are merely reversed.

The pivot is the beginning of the coiling action. It is the process of rotating the body clockwise and back, to gather impetus for the delivery. As mentioned before, the front or pivot foot should be slightly turned toward the third base line to better facilitate the pivot. The pivot foot is turned clockwise until it is parallel with the rubber as the body is turned toward third base. The pivot foot must not be lifted from the rubber. As the pivot is made, it is important to bend the back knee and thrust the pitching arm *down* to get the body ready for the powerful uncoiling action. (Illustration number 4.) In the lay back position with the knee bent, one of the key points is to have the back of the pitching hand facing up. This helps the pitcher's whip action and aids in guarding against pushing the ball. Stress

Illustration 4
Coiling Action

the reaching down technique rather than the reaching back technique. The pitcher's balance should be checked at this point to see if he can balance himself in this position without falling over.

There are three drills which will aid the pitcher in developing a strong coiling action. We refer to them as (1) the drinking glass drill, (2) the driving-the-arm-to-the ground drill and (3) the back-of-the-hand-up drill. These three helpful drills are described in chapter twelve. A loose, free, whip type delivery can be aided in its development by stressing the fundamentals of the coiling action and by using the recommended drills.

UNCOILING ACTION

The uncoiling action is the third part of our pitching form. The jack-in-the-box is pushed down and ready to spring but, unlike the jack-in-the-box, the catapulting action is forward rather than straight up. It is important, in order to generate the greatest amount of power that the uncoiling be controlled and efficient. Every move must come in its proper sequence. We will not burden you with the physiological sequence of movements but rather will present the most important elements that must be present in an efficient, powerful, uncoiling action.

The leg kick and the opening of the hips

As the uncoiling action begins, we find the pitcher turned toward third base, the pivot foot parallel with the rubber, the back knee bent, and the pitching arm thrust down, with the back of the hand up. The pitcher is now ready for the leg kick and the powerful opening of the hips. The size of the leg kick will vary with each individual pitcher. The pitcher should not kick so high that it ruins his balance, over-all coordination, and control. The leg is kicked up and rotated counter-clockwise (toward first base).

Illustration 5
Striding Across Center Line

The stride

The leg kick and opening of the hips begin the stride. The stride should not be over-emphasized. It should be thought of merely as a means to an end, as when a fighter steps to hit or a batter steps to hit. The stride should be natural and comfortable. Many young pitchers feel that the farther they stride the faster they will throw. This is not true. The stride should end on the balls of the feet not the heels. Landing on the heels jars the body and ruins the pitcher's control. The front leg should be bent upon ending the stride.

In order to make sure that the hips are opened fully and that the pitcher is not throwing against his body, his stride foot should land on, or to the first base side of an imaginary line drawn toward the plate from between the pitcher's feet. The back knee should be driven toward the ground as the stride is made.

The back should be loose and the body bent at the waist. (Illustration 6.)

Hip action

While we have already discussed opening the hips, for the sake of emphasis, it must be pointed out again that proper hip action is probably the greatest single factor involved in the powerful delivery. As in hitting, it is the place where a great amount of power is generated. Many have emphasized the push, we feel it is more important to stress the hip action. The hip action is strengthened by driving the back knee down as the hips are opened and the stride is completed. The hold-foot-back and the knee-to-ground drills are invaluable in stressing this important feature of the delivery. By the careful use of these drills the potency of the delivery can be greatly strengthened. Many of us have experienced the frustrations of watching a young pitcher's awkward movements, not knowing where to start in attempting to smooth them out. You will find it amazing how quickly these drills will improve the pitcher's over-all form. Do not overlook them—the results will be gratifying.

Illustration 6
Body Bend at Waist—Knee to Ground

Illustration 7
Follow-Through with Wrist

Follow-through and release

The follow-through should not be over-emphasized. It should be thought of as a natural culmination of a series of correct techniques in the delivery. As an example, the much practiced technique of having a pitcher bend to pick up an object at the end of his delivery to aid him in his follow-through is of little value if this is his main aim. Every other segment of his delivery could be wrong yet he could still pick up the object at the end of his delivery. If the coiling and uncoiling actions are correct (good pivot, bent back leg, loose bent back, correct opening of hips, striding on balls of feet across center line, staying on top of ball, etc.), the follow-through will be correct.

There are several additional points to be stressed that will help the follow-through and over-all delivery. The pitching arm should end up near the opposite knee with the palm of the hand facing toward the body. The back or pivot foot should end up opposite the striding foot with the weight balanced equally on each foot ready to field. You can aid the pitcher who has difficulty assuming this fielding position by having him take an additional small step with his stride foot to get his feet parallel.

The release point should be well out in front of the body. The pitcher should "think low" when releasing the ball. Slow motion films have proved that the ball is actually released some place near the pitcher's head but the pitcher must think about releasing it well out in front of him to achieve maximum efficiency. He must release the ball after coming over the top, with his fingers on top of the ball, as he imparts his wrist action, ending with the palm of the hand facing up (Illustration 7).

The pitcher must practice throwing over and over until he finds or feels his release point. A pitcher with a real feel knows when he has released the ball at the wrong point. This release point might be compared with the bowler releasing the ball out in front of him, rather than back by his leg.

FINGER ACTION AND GRIP

The correct finger action and grip will vary according to the type pitcher. The general principles of finger action and grip will be set forth in this section, but the specific fingering for different type pitches will be discussed in the chapters dealing with those pitches.

Finger pressure

Finger pressure is one of the major items that causes the ball to move. Some pitchers naturally have uneven finger pressure on the ball (one finger exerting more pressure than another). Thus the ball is caused to move in an irregular course.

Choosing the correct grip

All things being equal, the more seams that are rotating against the atmosphere the greater the action of the ball. The pitcher should strive to throw his best pitch with four seam rotation. When choosing the correct grip he should keep this principle in mind. All of the pitcher's pitches should be gripped in the same manner. He should not change his grip for each pitch. He should set his grip for his strong pitch.

Finding the proper grip for each pitcher is largely determined by adhering to the basic principles presented and, after much trial and error, ascertaining what is best for each pitcher. Getting the greatest amount of movement on the ball is the primary concern.

EXAMINING THE OVER-ALL FORM

We have divided the delivery into four basic segments: (1) preliminary actions, (2) coiling action, (3) uncoiling action and (4) finger action and grip. This was done for clarity of explanation only. The coach should not attempt to teach the proper form and delivery by using this breakdown as units of instruction, but he should be able to recognize the many segments of the delivery so as to better observe, diagnose, and suggest remedies for faults. The drills are also arranged in specific groupings to aid you in the instruction, but the pitcher should not be bothered in his learning with this division of segments.

The pitcher should be taught the *whole* form and delivery; if and when necessary, parts may be practiced, and then put back into the *whole* motion as discussed in chapter two. Remember, we do not want the pitcher to have to think about each minute detail and segment of his form and delivery.

To aid you in organizing your pitching instruction there is given a checklist of important points to stress in the development of the proper form and delivery:

1. The pitcher should throw *all* his pitches from the same angle.
2. The pitcher should not be forced into a delivery that is unnatural for him.
3. The pitcher must avoid *idiosyncrasies* that will "tip" his pitches. The ball should be held well up in the web of the glove, or if necessary the pitcher should wind up with the ball in the glove.
4. The pitcher should vary his motion by varying his pumps and taking varied amounts of time between pitches so that the batter will be unable to hit off his rhythm.
5. The eyes should remain constantly fixed on the target throughout the delivery.
6. The pitching arm should be thrust down with the back of the hand up, as he drives down to pitch.
7. Hip action is one of the most important aspects to be stressed in the delivery.
8. The back should be bent and loose in the delivery.
9. The leg kick and stride should not be exaggerated.
10. The follow-through should be a natural culmination of the total form and delivery.
11. The hand and wrist action should be loose and flexible.

12. The stride leg should land on the ball of the foot, on or across the center line.
13. The pitcher must practice to find *his* proper release point and keep it consistently.
14. The ball should be gripped loosely but firmly in the fingers. The ball should not be choked back in the palm of the hand.
15. The grip should be selected, bearing in mind the four seam rotation principle, the pitcher's best pitch, and the pitcher's type of delivery.

By following closely the methods indicated and the suggested drills which are presented in chapter twelve, many of the difficulties which are always encountered in building the pitcher's form and delivery can be dealt with successfully.

◆ The Fast Ball

five

In the first chapter we stated that the pitcher with the over-powering fast ball possesses an important gift but that the possession of this gift does not guarantee him success. We also mentioned that the young pitcher without this gift is not doomed to defeat. These are interesting statements, but what do they mean? How can the pitcher with the overpowering fast ball best make use of this gift? How can a pitcher without this overpowering fast ball be successful? In this chapter we will answer these questions and present the principles and methods that can best be employed to get the maximum results from your pitcher's natural resources.

The good fast ball is more than a ball that is moving at a rapid rate of speed. Many infielders for example, can throw the ball hard but are not effective when they get on the mound. The good fast ball must be alive, it must hop, sink, break, sail or move from its straight trajectory. A good fast ball is not a straight ball. Some pitcher's fast balls move naturally and some pitchers have to work hard to *make* their fast balls move. Many young pitchers in their anxiety to learn a variety of different pitches do not spend enough time on improving their fast ball. They take their fast ball for granted. There is more to throwing a good fast ball than just trying to throw the ball as hard as you can.

IMPORTANCE OF THE FAST BALL

Most batters are instructed to be ready to hit the fast ball and have the curve ball in mind. To be effective the pitcher must gain the batter's respect for his fast ball. To make his other pitches effective the pitcher must have at least an adequate fast ball. It is the pitch that keeps the hitter from digging in and getting set for the pitcher's curve, change-of-pace or other specialty pitches. If the hitter must set himself for the fast ball it will make the other pitches more effective.

The fast ball is the most important pitch for the young pitcher to develop. He must learn to throw it with control when and where he wants.

He should master his fast ball before trying to learn the other pitches. The chances of a pitcher being successful without a dependable fast ball are not very good.

TWO SCHOOLS OF THOUGHT

There are two general schools of thought regarding the fast ball: The either-you-have-it-or-you-don't school and the fast-ball-can-be-helped school.

The either-you-have-it-or-you-don't school

This group claims that either a boy is born with a fast ball or he is not. There is not much hope for the boy who is not. They claim the same for hitters, feeling that hitters are born, not developed. Let us look at some of the determinants of the born fast ball pitcher.

Body build. The tall lean boy with the long arms and big hands is considered to have a better chance of being gifted with the outstanding fast ball than the shorter, stocky type pitcher.

Size of muscles. The born fast ball pitcher usually has long sinewy muscles.

Flexibility. The good fast ball pitcher has a loose flexible arm and a loose wrist which propels the ball in a whiplike action.

Coordination. The pitcher must be well-coordinated so that his body performs efficiently in delivering the ball at top speed.

The natural born fast ball pitcher, according to the foregoing should be about six feet four inches tall, weigh about one-hundred and ninety pounds, have long arms and big hands, long sinewy muscles, a loose flexible arm and wrist, and be exceptionally well-coordinated.

It is agreed that these are important characteristics to look for in a pitcher with a good fast ball, but few possess all of them.

The fast-ball-can-be-helped school

Coaches must belong to this school or we are in the wrong business. The majority of high school coaches find themselves with pitchers far below the caliber described in the above paragraphs. You must make the best use of the material you get. Even if you are fortunate enough to have a pitcher of exceptional ability, you owe it to the boy to help him develop into an outstanding pitcher. Even the ideal pitcher described in the preceding paragraphs can be helped. Raw physical ability alone will not do the job.

Some baseball men are prone to say, "Let the boy alone; he will develop. I had to learn the hard way." We do not agree. We feel our job is to try to speed up the learning process, not merely to let the boy flounder around wasting precious time in his development. I am afraid in many cases the let-him-alone coach is covering up for lack of knowledge. We do agree, however, that if you do not know what to do it is best to let the boy alone. The young pitcher's career can easily be hurt by a well-meaning but misinformed pitching coach.

Before going into the various ways of helping to develop the fast ball, it would be well to prove that a fast ball can be helped.

MAKING UP FOR PHYSICAL DEFICIENCIES

A boy these days is not doomed to being weak. It used to be that if a pitcher was skinny and weak there was no hope for him to be a powerful pitcher. As we learned in chapter three, there are many accepted ways to strengthen the young pitchers.

We can strengthen his legs, trunk, shoulders, neck, arms, wrists, and fingers, thus making him a stronger pitcher. After analyzing the pitcher's weaknesses it is necessary to help strengthen him at these points through exercises and drills.

Besides the program outlined in chapter three, one of the best ways to strengthen a pitcher's fast ball is to have him throw as much as possible. As the best way to strengthen the legs for running is through running, the best way to strengthen the arm for throwing is through throwing.

If the young pitcher will follow the program outlined in chapter three, and work diligently to strengthen his throwing arm, he will be able to develop a lot of the characteristics that the natural born fast ball pitcher is blessed with. It is true that some boys naturally will be able to throw harder than others but this does not mean that each boy should not be encouraged to improve upon his deficiencies thus allowing him to attain his own personal optimum performance. You must leave no stone unturned in helping your pitchers reach their maximum potential.

IMPROVING THE FAST BALL

The fast ball can be improved by adhering to certain basic fundamentals. In discussing improvement in this section we are emphasizing improving the velocity, movement, or liveness of the fast ball. As the young pitcher develops and his arm grows stronger, you will have to determine whether he is the natural, hopping, fast ball type pitcher, or the type who needs a little cunning to make his fast ball move. Both types *need* help and *can* be helped.

The hopping fast ball pitcher

The hopping fast ball pitcher is the hard throwing, overhand or three-quarter pitcher. To make the ball hop, the pitcher must give backspin to the ball. We call this the six-to-twelve counter-clockwise rotation. Some pitcher's fast balls naturally hop more than others, but this live action can be improved upon.

Illustration 8
12 to 6 Rotation
Down Breaking Curve

Illustration 8
6 to 12 Rotation
Backspin—Hopping Fast Ball

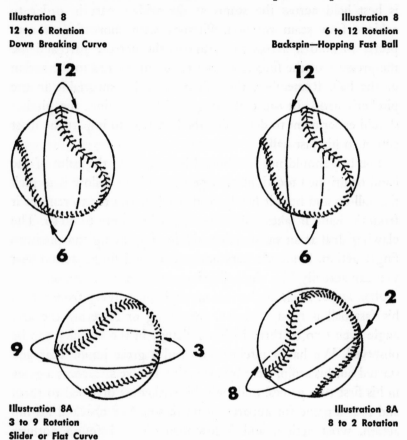

Illustration 8A
3 to 9 Rotation
Slider or Flat Curve

Illustration 8A
8 to 2 Rotation

Rotation. Many times a young pitcher's fast ball gets hit because it is not rotating properly. It may have a slider spin or off-center spin (two-to-eight rotation) which slows down the velocity and makes the ball easier to hit. This off-center spin is usually the result of holding the ball off-center or not getting on top of the ball. If the index and middle finger are spread on the ball this often causes poor fast ball rotation. You can observe this poor rotation by standing in back of the catcher.

Fingering. To get maximum six-to-twelve rotation the ball is best held across the seams at the widest part in order to achieve four seam rotation. Pitchers with short fingers may prefer to hold it across the seams at the narrow part and use the pressure of the fingers against the seams to add to the action of the ball. Remember, the ball must feel comfortable in the pitcher's hand. In the early stages of his learning, the pitcher should experiment to determine the best way to impart the most action to his fast ball.

The ball should not be choked back toward the palm of the hand or gripped too tightly. A general rule to follow is to pick the ball up and hold it firmly so that when you try to remove it from the hand it takes a slight amount of pressure to do so. The clawing drill is an outstanding aid for improving the pitcher's finger action. Some pitchers have such good finger action that you can actually hear the ball being clawed as it is released.

Arm angle. Each pitcher has an angle of delivery from which his fast ball is most effective. By raising or lowering the arm angle even two or three inches a change in the velocity can be observed. We had a pitcher who had a great junior year and started out his senior year by averaging twelve strikeouts a game in his first two games. Suddenly his strikeouts dropped to three and four a game for apparently no reason. We checked his hip action, wrist action, and follow-through, and found nothing wrong. It was three weeks before we noticed that he had raised his arm angle about four inches, thus slipping out of his natural whip-like groove. This new angle and impairment of his natural coordination had cost him a great amount of action on his fast ball. We experimented in practice and found whenever he raised his arm he began to get hit and the lack of action on his fast ball was quite noticeable. With each new pitcher you will have to experiment to find the best angle of delivery. This is an important factor not to be overlooked.

Over-all form. Form and delivery were covered thoroughly in chapter four. There are some major points, however, that should be emphasized again when trying to improve the fast ball.

The wrist and arm should be flexible and the back of the hand should be facing up in the lay-back position to produce a good hip action. The drinking glass drill is a fine aid in developing flexible wrist action. (Illustration 9.)

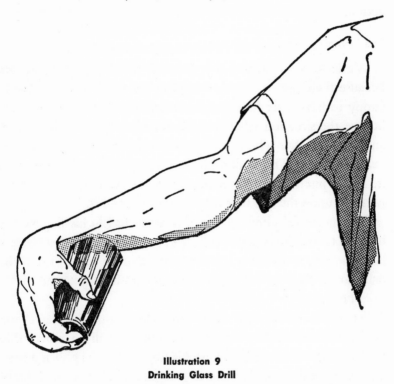

Illustration 9
Drinking Glass Drill

Many times a pitcher is not getting the most out of his fast ball because he is not opening his hips properly. He must stride across the imaginary center line when delivering the pitch. If the pitcher does not open his hips, a smooth, powerful, delivery is impeded. The hip action can be helped by driving the back knee toward the ground as the stride is made. The holding-the-foot-back drill is also a valuable aid in improving the hip action.

The back should be loose and bent during the delivery. A low release point should be stressed. The chest-on-knee drill will aid the pitcher in emphasizing bending his back. (Illustration 6 page 84.) As the pitcher ends his follow-through, the palm of his hand should be facing him to guarantee maximum wrist action.

The "cunning" fast ball pitcher

We have seen pitchers that baseball men have given up on, because their fast ball did not hop, it was dead. We are always happy to have a six foot four inch fireballer but must make the best of the situation when we are not blessed with this type of animal. A pitcher who is willing to work can learn to make his fast ball move. This is done by exerting uneven pressure upon it. Many pitchers do this naturally, some exerting such uneven pressure upon the ball that they cannot control it.

The successful pitcher must have good feel in his fingers and be able to manipulate the ball with his fingers. By applying a little more pressure with one finger or another he can make the ball move. The pitcher can experiment until he gets the directions he wants.

Perhaps the foregoing seems somewhat vague. But have you ever asked an old pitcher how he got his ball to move? He probably answered, talking with his fingers, "Oh! I give it a little of this and a little of that and it goes like this." Not much help! We will try to be more specific.

We have had success in making the fast ball move by following through with the hand and wrist moving toward the glove hand rather than straight toward the ground. Pressure is applied with the index finger, to the inside of the ball imparting an eight-to-two spin. This action causes the ball to sink or move in on the batter. The inward turning of the wrist is not over-emphasized as in the screwball. To make the technique more clear let us set up a step by step procedure. This procedure is only for hand and wrist action in your right hand.

Step one. Hold the ball in your right hand about six inches in front of your nose with the back of your hand and the back of the index and middle fingers facing you as an Indian does when he says, "How!"

Step two. The normal follow-through of the hand for a hopping fast ball would be from your nose, on a straight line down past your chin. Instead of this, as your right hand gets down to chin level exert moderate pressure with your index finger toward the left releasing the ball.

Step three. With your left hand grasp your right wrist in the starting position and practice imparting the eight-to-two spin to a partner three feet away.

Step four. As you become competent at imparting the spin, practice throwing from twenty to thirty feet using your normal delivery. Check the spin; if it is good, pitch from the normal distance. From time to time you will lose the spin and then you must go back and start the procedure over to strengthen the habit.

This pitch can easily be learned. Try it, and then have your pitchers try it, the results will amaze you. Some pitchers may find it easier to accomplish if they spread their fingers slightly on the ball.

Some of our pitchers have had success making the ball move by holding it with the seams, or off-center with the middle finger on one seam. Again, the pitcher will have to experiment to find the best way to make his fast ball move.

SPEED VARIATIONS ON THE FAST BALL

Very few pitchers throw hard enough to throw the ball past the hitter when he is set for it. A pitcher with mediocre speed *can* throw the ball past the hitter if he is expecting another type pitch or a different speed pitch. If the pitcher throws as hard as he can on every pitch the hitters will eventually time his fast ball and be able to hit him.

The 90% fast ball and the 98% fast ball

We like our advanced pitchers to be able to throw at least two different speed fast balls. We call his regular fast ball his 90% fast ball and his extra fast ball his 98% fast ball. We use 98% rather than 100% because we feel he must pitch under control and we feel that in a 100% effort, body control and balance are often forfeited.

The ability of a pitcher to differentiate between his regular fast ball and his extra fast ball is often the difference between a mediocre pitcher and a great one. You must guard against your pitcher letting up and dropping his regular fast ball to 80% and thinking that his 90% fast ball is his extra fast ball. Remember, his 98% fast ball must have something *extra* on it. This takes patience and practice and must be worked on conscientiously. Have your pitcher throw his regular assortment of pitches as you are working with him and from time to time call for his 98% fast ball. Analyze it and ask the batter, catcher, and pitcher if they noticed the difference. The outstanding fast ball pitcher must possess the extra fast ball.

Setting up the extra fast ball

We do not wish to confuse the issue at this time and discuss all the different ways the pitcher can set up the extra fast ball. We are concerned at this point with the relationship between the 90% fast ball and the 98% fast ball. Let us use a hypothetical situation to illustrate the idea.

The batter comes up the first time with no one on base and the pitcher shows him the 90% fast ball and he eventually flys out, hitting the 90% fast ball. The next time up, the bases are loaded in a crucial situation and the pitcher has a one and two count on the hitter. He wants to strike the batter out. He shows the batter his 90% fast ball but makes sure it is thrown for a ball. With the count two and two and the batter thinking he has seen the fast ball and has timed it, the pitcher reaches back and throws the 98% or extra fast ball past the batter. The principle is to make the batter think he knows your fast ball and then at the opportune time give him the extra fast ball for which he is not ready. We had a pitcher who won fourteen games for us one year who only threw eight or nine of these 98% fast balls per game, the number depending on the situations occurring in the game. Some baseball men felt that this pitcher was not a prospect because he did not throw extra hard on every pitch. This boy was interested in becoming a pitcher, not just a hard thrower, and by making use of his two fast balls, a fair curve, and a change-of-pace, he became the top high school ball player in the country and signed a professional contract for a sizeable bonus.

WHERE TO THROW THE FAST BALL

Again, you must classify your pitcher. Is he a hopping fast ball pitcher, a sinking or breaking fast ball pitcher, a side-armer, a control pitcher, or a wild pitcher?

The "hopping" fast ball pitcher

This pitcher's fast ball has backspin and hops or rises. We recommend that these pitchers try to keep everything low. Some of these pitchers, however, have met with success by throwing their fast ball high and their curve low. The different pitching strategies will be dealt with in detail in chapter nine. We recommend, especially for the beginning pitcher, that he keep his mind on throwing low.

The "sinking" or "breaking" fast ball pitcher

This type pitcher *must* keep his fast ball low and, in most situations, away from the hitter. There may be situations when he wants to jam the hitter especially if his fast ball has a tendency to move in. He may help his ball move in by letting it slide off the ends of his index and middle fingers.

The side-arm fast ball

The effectiveness of the side-armer is largely based on his ability to set the batter back on his heels and get him to lean away from the pitch. He *must* keep this pitch outside. If he gets the pitch inside the hitter has a chance to kill it, even though he is leaning away from the pitch. Many a side-armer has bit the dust because he could not keep his pitch outside. The side-arm fast ball has a tendency to sink, so should generally be kept low.

The control pitcher and the wildman

The control pitcher may use any of several plans in setting up the hitters. He can pitch in and out, high and low, or everything low, and can afford to waste more pitches to set the hitter up. The wildman must throw the majority of his pitches down the middle and hope that his stuff takes care of the corners. Control and strategy are discussed in detail in chapters eight and nine respectively.

Let us now, in reference to the fast ball, consider various drills. These drills are very important in teaching the fast ball. We have included detailed descriptions of each drill in chapter twelve but for ease of reference we will list them here:

1. Weighted ball drill. (To strengthen hands, wrists, and fingers)
2. Clawing ball drill. (To improve finger action)
3. Drinking glass drill. (To improve wrist action)
4. Center-line drill. (To improve over-all form)
5. Knee-to-ground drill. (To improve hip action)
6. Holding-foot-back drill. (To improve hip action)
7. Chest-on-knee drill. (To help bend back)
8. Holding-wrist drill. (To develop finger action and to concentrate on rotation)
9. Hand-to-hand drill. (To develop rotation)
10. Ten foot drill. (To develop rotation)

THE CHANGE-OF-PACE OFF THE FAST BALL

The change-of-pace is probably the most overlooked pitch in the young pitcher's repertoire. Even those pitchers who spend much time in practice on the change-of-pace often neglect its use in the heat of battle. The pitcher must have confidence in his change and to gain this confidence he has to throw it until it becomes a part of his pitching pattern. In the development stage we demand that our pitchers throw at least three changes an inning to help establish the habit. A good change-of-pace can make an outstanding pitcher out of an otherwise mediocre one.

Ingredients of the change-of-pace

The change-of-pace off the fast ball must be thrown so that it looks like a fast ball. The pitcher is depending on the element of surprise for its success. He must make sure he does not tip his pitch. He must practice and practice until the motion used for the change is exactly the same as that used for the fast ball. The pitcher must avoid the obvious slowing of the body or arm action in throwing the change. Some pitchers are guilty of grimacing or changing their facial expression when throwing this pitch. Do not let your pitcher over-act when throwing the change-of-pace.

The change-of-pace must be kept low. The pitch should not be too slow but just slow enough to throw the hitter off stride.

Teaching the change-of-pace

Some young pitchers claim they throw their change by palming the ball while others may claim they throw it by dragging their back foot or by holding it back. We teach that the good change-of-pace is the combination of proper grip, hand, wrist, and arm action and correct body action.

The grip. Have your pitcher grip the ball imagining that the tips of his middle and index fingers are cut-off. The tips of the fingers are held off the ball and the ball is held by the second joints. (Illustration 10.) As the young pitcher masters this technique he can lay the tips on the ball so as not to give the pitch away but he must exert no pressure with the tips of his fingers. The ball is choked back in the hand more than it would be in throwing the fast ball.

The hand, wrist, and arm action. The ball is released with the hand behind the ball rather than on top as in throwing the fast

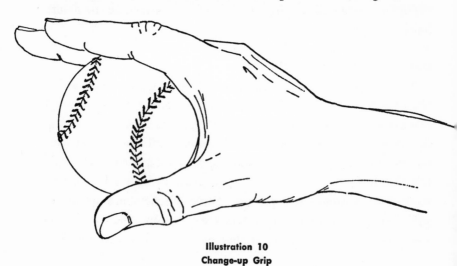

Illustration 10
Change-up Grip

ball. The wrist is dead and the pitcher should simulate pulling down a window shade as he pitches.

Correct body action. Most pitchers will have to limit their body action to some extent in throwing the change-of-pace. In the early teaching, have the pitcher throw his change while holding his back foot on the rubber. As he develops the pitch he can release the ball and let his foot come forward so as not to tip the pitch. It amounts to a slight hesitation of the body action, thus keeping the pitcher from getting full body impetus into the pitch. A low release point must be stressed; with the hand behind the ball the pitcher will find that he has to exaggerate the low release point to keep the ball low.

Purpose of the change-of-pace

We want the batter to hit the change-of-pace. We want him to hit it off balance and pop it up or hit it into the ground. It must be thrown for a strike. It is a good pitch when he is behind in the count and it can serve to get him out of the hole.

If the pitcher is getting hit solidly, he might resort to the change to throw the hitters' timing off, rather than try to throw harder and harder as many pitchers do. The change-of-pace is also effective when used after a batter has fouled off two or three fast balls.

You will have to sell your pitchers on the importance of the change-of-pace. The average young pitcher seems to get more thrill out of buzzing the fast ball or breaking off the big curve. A method of salesmanship we have used is to have the pitcher throw only fast balls and change-ups to the batters in batting practice and point out how inept the batters are at getting good wood on the ball. The batters will usually help make the point with their complaints to the pitcher to quit changing speeds.

♦ The Curve Ball

six

The curve ball *can* be taught. By following a systematic method of instruction, teaching the curve ball can be one of the most satisfying experiences in coaching. In many activities it is difficult for the coach or teacher to determine whether he is really getting his information over to his students. This is not so when teaching the pitcher how to throw the curve because the results of the improvement can be observed each day as you watch the break in the curve ball increase.

Through trial and error, experimentation and research, we have devised a simple step-by-step approach to teaching the curve ball. This method has proved successful with both beginning and advanced pitchers. With patience, careful application of the methods prescribed, and a little time on your part, the coach can develop good curve-ball pitchers.

IMPORTANCE OF THE CURVE BALL

In chapter five we explained that a pitcher could not get by on his fast ball alone, but would need a change-of-pace to throw the batter off stride. By adding the curve to his repertory the pitcher is forcing the batter to contend with the vertical and horizontal movement of the ball as well as with the speed and deception on the straight plane that is accomplished with the fast ball and the change-of-pace. The curve ball has long been recognized as the "great equalizer." Many a rookie hitter has written, "Be home soon Ma, they're starting to curve me."

THE GOOD CURVE BALL

The good curve ball is the down-breaking curve. We are not interested in the flat or "nickle" curve that so many young pitchers throw. The flat curve is easy to hit because it comes up to the batter on a flat plane and he does not have to contend with the vertical action of the ball. The flat curve is caused by dropping the elbow and releasing the ball off the outside of the index finger in a counter clockwise motion (three-to-nine rotation).

The good curve is thrown with a high elbow, the ball being released over the top of the index finger in a twelve-to-six clockwise downward rotation. By top of the index finger, we are referring to the top edge of the finger, not the tip. (Illustration 11.) The method used to throw the down-breaking curve is not hard on the arm, as is the method used to throw the nickle

Illustration 11
Curve Ball Release over Top of Index Finger

curve. The successful curve ball pitcher must be able to make the curve break down, at different speeds, and with different amounts of break. These techniques *can* be learned.

OVER-ALL VIEW OF THE CURVE BALL

The rotation or spin of the ball against the atmosphere causes the ball to curve. The faster the rotation the greater the curve. The ball will curve in the direction it is rotating. Learning to spin the ball is the most important part of learning to throw the curve because without good rotation the pitcher can never develop a good curve ball.

After the pitcher has achieved good rotation he must develop the curve ball motion. Rotation alone will not produce the good curve; it must be accompanied by proper body action. The successful curve ball pitcher has good curve ball rhythm.

Our approach to teaching the curve ball might be compared with the approach of the insurance salesman. He is not concerned in the beginning with selling you a policy but only with the problem of getting his foot in the door. From there he hopes to gain your friendship and confidence, discuss your needs for insurance and eventually sell you the policy. In teaching the curve ball we do not start by throwing a curve sixty feet or by explaining the entire curve ball process. We begin with finger action and rotation, and then proper arm, hand, and body action, eventually reaching our goal of the finished curve ball. The good curve ball is the result of superbly coordinated action from the toes to the finger tips.

STEP ONE: GRIP

We stated earlier that the grip should be the same for each pitch, i.e., the fast ball, change, curve, and specialty pitches, should all be held in the same way so that the pitch will not be tipped. Determine the pitcher's strongest pitch and have him grip all the pitches the way he grips his strongest one. The ideal is to get four seam rotation because the more seams that rotate against the atmosphere the greater the movement of the ball. Have the pitcher hold his fast ball across the wide part of the seams and then have him turn the ball a quarter turn so that his middle finger is resting along the seam. (Illustration 12.) This is the ideal fingering as it allows the pitcher four seam rotation on both the fast ball and curve and he can apply good finger action to the curve by exerting pressure with the middle finger on the seam. If the pitcher tries this conscientiously and it does not feel good to him, do not force him but let him experiment to find the best way for *him*.

Finger tip control is very important in throwing the curve ball. The pitcher's fingers must learn to *feel* the curve ball. The ball should be gripped loosely but firmly, well out in the fingers because choking the ball back in the palm will impede the spinning action and fine feel of the curve. Most of the pressure for the curve is applied by the middle finger and thumb as the ball is released *over* the index finger.

STEP TWO: IMPARTING ROTATION

This is the most important aspect in throwing the curve ball. We want the ball to rotate in the twelve-to-six, downward direction.

Have the pitcher hold the ball in front of him below chest height using the proper grip with his index and middle fingers on top of the ball and his thumb underneath. The ball is held in the right hand with the hand cocked toward the left. From this position, the pitcher spins the ball as fast as he can, rotating the hand so that the index and middle finger end up on the bottom of the ball and the thumb on the top. (Illustration 13.) The pitcher must do this over and over until the ball is spinning at a good rate of speed in the twelve-to-six direction. The pitcher

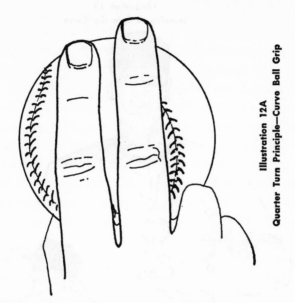

Illustration 12A
Quarter Turn Principle—Curve Ball Grip

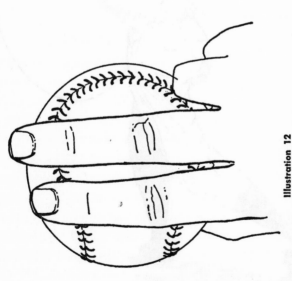

Illustration 12
Fast Ball Across Seams Grip
Before Quarter Turn For Curve

Illustration 13
Learning to Spin the Curve

Illustration 14
Throwing the Curve over and Around the Barrel

should not try to go any further until he has mastered this spin. To help make this a habit, we have the pitcher practice the T.V. drill every chance he gets. (Drill no. 14.) In this drill he clicks his thumb and middle finger without the ball, with the same hand action described above. He should do this during the day when he has nothing else to do.

When the pitcher has demonstrated that he has this simple spinning technique mastered we proceed to the hand to hand drill. (Drill no. 11.) The elbow is raised slightly higher than the shoulder and the hand is bent in toward the ear. The ball is rotated over the top of the index finger and caught in the left hand. In this drill the whole arm is rotated at the shoulder and the elbow is kept high.

These two steps lay the ground work for the good curve ball. The process should not be a hurried one. There is a great temptation to rush on to the next step even though the pitcher has not completely mastered the previous one. Do not succumb to this temptation, remember, one step at a time. We have even taught the first step in rotating the ball to an eight-year-old girl.

STEP THREE: THROWING THE ROTATING BALL

Our next procedure is to throw the ball ten feet to a partner using the same technique explained in the hand to hand drill. The elbow *must* be up and the hand turned in at a right angle, toward the ear.

Next, we throw the ball ten feet using the full pitching motion paying particular attention to the few basic fundamentals already covered. The ball must be thrown easily and in a looping motion. (Drill no. 12.)

We are now ready to add a few refinements. The pitcher should attempt to get *himself* on top of the ball. He should have the feeling he is over the ball looking down on it. This action can be helped by taking a very short stride. You should also stress the pulling down action as the ball is released. This action might be likened to skidding the tires in the mud. The ball should be released with the back of the hand facing the batter. For the sake of clarity, before going into the next phase, we list the principles established thus far:

1. Four seam rotation, if possible (quarter-turn principle).
2. Finger tip control.
3. Twelve-to-six clockwise rotation with the ball being released *over the top* of the index finger.
4. Pressure application with the middle finger and thumb.
5. Faster rotation (the better the curve).
6. Hand turned in, elbow high.
7. Whole shoulder rotation with the pitch.
8. Being on top of the ball.
9. Skidding tire action.

STEP FOUR: CURVE BALL BODY ACTION

The pitcher must develop curve ball rhythm. His curve ball cannot be thrown hard or awkwardly, but rather with a smooth motion. This is often the hardest part for the beginner to master.

When the pitcher has mastered the rotation, you can explain to him that the curve must be thrown smoothly and that he should try to get on top of the ball. With these two instructions, turn him loose to throw the curve. Now is the time to allow him to experiment a little on his own. The method of rotation had to be regimented, but the body action is somewhat different for each person and should not be regimented. After he has experimented and done some adjustment your job is one of refinement.

Re-check the basic fundamentals to see that they are being followed. Point out the major faults, worry about the minor ones later. Remember to point out the good points as well as the bad. Encourage your pitcher.

One of the most common faults of poor curve ball action is

over-striding. If anything, have him exaggerate a short stride in this beginning period. This will help him get on top of the ball.

There are many ways to get crucial points over to your pitchers. It is up to the successful coach to have a storehouse of word pictures and gimmicks to use when the need arises. Some aids will work for one pitcher but will not help another at all. We have two illustrations that have met with considerable success when dealing with the curve ball motion. One we call the sack-over-the-shoulder idea which is very simple. We have the pitcher imagine that he is reaching back over his shoulder to pick up a heavy sack with both hands and then he slowly brings the sack over his shoulder to the ground in front of him. This action is almost an exact copy of the curve ball motion and if the pitcher can feel this it will help him considerably.

The barrel

Over the years we have tried to come up with one general idea that would serve to illustrate the curve ball motion. We were looking for something that could be used to describe all facets of the motion without going into great detail. We finally came up with the barrel idea. We have been very pleased with the results brought about by its use.

The barrel is an imaginary one which the pitcher sees in front of him about six inches above his head and continuing down to the knees. (Illustration 14.) As you read this, imagine along with us as if you were the pitcher. The pitcher must actually see this barrel in his mind. As he throws the curve he goes up the front, over the top, out around the barrel and pulls up underneath as he follows through—the ideal curve ball action. If you follow this process you will see there is no room for faulty technique. To point out more precisely how the barrel technique works some of its uses are listed:

1. If the motion is too fast and jerky the hand will go through the barrel rather than over and around it.
2. If the stride is too long it will pull the arm and hand through the barrel.
3. Going over and around helps keep the arm and hand out away from the body.
4. Going over and around keeps the motion at the right speed.
5. Going over helps the proper angle of delivery.
6. Going around and under helps the pull and follow-through.

These are only a few of the advantages of the barrel technique. As you try it you will discover more and different ways to use it. Its greatest strength is its self-explanatory nature. You do not have to point out each minute detail of the delivery but only have to paint the picture and the techniques must fall in line. It is a helpful aid when used in correcting flaws in the delivery as we shall point out later on.

Before continuing our chapter on the curve ball we should like to emphasize a point that has already been made. *The curve ball can be taught.* Do not underestimate the methods described. They have been proved to work and do not take much experience on the part of the coach. Read the explanations over again and try them. The results will be very satisfying.

ANALYZING THE PITCHER FOR COMMON FAULTS

One of the major tasks of the coach is to correct mistakes and flaws as they occur. Suddenly, the ball is not breaking correctly or the curve is hanging and the pitcher comes to you asking, "Why?" The successful coach must be able to help the pitcher in this dilemma. To aid you in meeting this problem we present the major faults that are forever cropping up among pitchers who are trying to throw the curve ball. For simplicity of presentation we have divided the faults into three sections, (1) lack of good twelve-to-six rotation, (2) the "hanging" curve and, (3) the bouncing curve.

Lack of good twelve-to-six downward rotation

The pitcher's rotation should be checked in the same sequence that we presented the teaching of proper rotation i.e., spin in front of the chest, hand to hand rotation, ten foot rotation and full distance rotation. If the ball is not rotating properly it is easy for you as coach to discover. There will usually be a "button" visible on the ball as it spins toward the plate. The red seams spinning off center give an illusion of a button on the ball which means the pitcher is not getting a good twelve-to-six rotation. In the following paragraphs the major causes of poor rotation are presented.

Not releasing the ball over the top of the index finger. If the ball is released off the side of the index finger rather than over the top the result will be a three-to-nine spin. It is imperative that the curve be released over the top of the index finger with the back of the hand facing the plate.

Wrist not turned in. The wrist should be cocked in toward the ear in the delivery. As the pitcher gains in experience he can straighten the hand out more but we emphasize keeping the hand in at first in order to get away from the flat curve which is the result of turning the hand counter clockwise and releasing the ball off the side of the index finger.

Elbow not held high. If the elbow is dropped, the result is a flattening out of the curve. Many a pitcher in the late innings will grow arm weary and inadvertently drop his elbow several inches in delivering the curve and the curve flattens out. You must constantly caution your pitcher to keep his elbow high because with a high elbow it is almost impossible to throw a flat curve.

Poor finger action. From the beginning, strong finger action must be stressed. The T.V. drill and all the spinning drills must be practiced constantly to insure strong finger action.

Gripping the ball too tightly. If the ball is gripped too tightly the rotation of the ball is retarded because the fingers are not allowed to work freely to impart good spin to the ball. If the rotation looks slow to you, there is a good chance the ball is being held too tightly.

Gripping the ball too far back in the hand. If the ball is "choked" too far back in the hand, the spin will be smothered so that proper rotation cannot be accomplished.

The hanging curve

The hanging curve is a curve ball that tends to stay up in the batter's eyes rather than break sharply down. This is one of the easiest pitches for the batter to hit. The common causes of the hanging curve are presented in the following paragraphs.

Not pulling down hard enough. After the hand reaches the top of the barrel the pitcher should pull down hard as his hand goes around and under the barrel. If he does not pull hard the ball will have a tendency to hang.

Not getting on top of the ball. The pitcher must get on top of the ball to keep it from hanging. It often helps to shorten his stride to do so. It is impossible to get on top of the ball if the stride is too long. If the pitcher comes to the top of the barrel and releases the ball he is not getting on top of the ball. He must go over, around, and under the barrel. He must guard against releasing the ball too soon.

Not bending the back. The back must be bent as the pitcher goes around the barrel. The chest-to-knee drill is a good aid for proper back action.

Quick remedy for the hanging curve. If the curve is hanging and you do not know what to do, have the pitcher take about a one foot stride and throw a soft curve. We have found this often restores the curve ball because it forces the pitcher to get on top and also helps the rotation.

The bouncing curve

By bouncing curve, we refer to the curve ball that looks as if it is thrown right into the ground. We are *not* referring to the curve ball that is purposely "broken" on the plate as a waste pitch or as a result of missing on a knee high attempt. The bouncing curve is often caused by hurrying the motion. The sack-over-shoulder illustration will help remedy this situation.

Poor over-all curve ball rhythm will cause the curve to bounce. This is usually observed in the jerky uncoordinated action of the pitcher. If the pitcher comes to the top of the barrel and cuts across it rather than using a full motion around it, the result will be a bouncing curve. The pitcher must take his time, be smooth, and go over, around, and under the barrel to throw a good curve ball.

IMPROVING THE CURVE BALL

When the pitcher has mastered the fundamentals of throwing the curve ball, you can begin to help him improve upon it. He should be helped to analyze himself, to throw different breaking curves at different speeds, and to know where and when to throw the curve.

Analyzing the curve ball pitcher

You and the pitcher will have to decide whether he is going to be a predominately curve ball pitcher, or a fast ball pitcher who uses the curve to keep the batter honest.

The pitcher who relies on his curve ball as his best pitch should have several different types of curves in his repertory. The pitcher can learn to throw different type curves. The important principle is to make his curves look alike until the last instant. If the pitcher has shown his regular curve it is imperative that his extra curve come up in the same way and then break more sharply, surprising the batter. This is the mark of a good curve ball pitcher.

The fast ball pitcher who uses his curve to keep the batter honest must be able to throw the good curve for strikes and also will want to be able to throw it to spots. He will have to fit his curve ball into his general pitching pattern. In general, he will want to throw his curve low, no matter whether he is a high fast ball pitcher, an in-and-out pitcher, or an everything-low pitcher. He should have enough confidence in his curve to be able to use it occasionally when he is behind in the count thereby keeping the batter honest.

You must be able to analyze the pitcher's progress. As he strives for perfection, he must reach the point where he can throw a good rotating curve without giving it too much thought. We might compare the pitcher with the motorist in heavy traffic, who has no time for analyzing his clutch action or shifting action; he must do this unconsciously while he concentrates on the traffic. In the same manner, the pitcher cannot be conscious of every physical action involved in throwing the curve, it must be thrown from habit as he concentrates more fully on getting the batter out. Until the pitcher has learned to throw the curve from habit he is not a finished product. Analyze his form periodically for flaws that can be corrected and improvements that can be made. Do not be so critical that you ruin the pitcher's confidence. Encourage him!

Different breaks at different speeds

It is easy to change the speed and break of the curve when the pitcher has been taught in the beginning to throw it with the hand turned in. Raise your elbow slightly higher than your shoulder and bend the hand toward the ear as far as you can. The farther the hand is turned in, the slower the curve and the bigger the break. With the hand turned in at a maximum the result will be a slow rainbow curve. The curve can also be slowed up by holding the ball farther back in the fingers but this is not always necessary or desirable. The slow, big breaking, curve is very effective when mixed in with the fast curve.

To help you understand our principle, place your hand and arm in the position mentioned above and imagine that your index finger is the trigger finger on a gun. Slowly raise the trigger finger toward the ceiling by straightening the hand until it is in a straight line with your forearm. (Illustration 15.) This extreme will give the pitcher the fast, smaller breaking curve. Any angle of the hand between the two extremes will change the speed and break of the ball.

Important rule

The inside, or little finger side of the forearm should always be facing the batter when throwing the curve. (Shaded area of illustration 15A.) It is impossible to throw a flat, nickel curve if this simple rule is followed. The speed of the curve can also be aided by holding the ball farther out in the fingers and increasing the wrist snap.

Where and when to throw the curve

In most cases the curve should be thrown low and away. If the curve gets up high it is easy to hit. The pitcher must concentrate on a low target at all times. If he concentrates on releasing the ball around and under the barrel he will be able to keep the ball low consistently. Another guide that helps the pitcher keep the ball low is to have him end up with his pitching hand next to his opposite knee when finishing his follow-through. He must concentrate on bending his back and getting on top and over the barrel. The down-breaking curve is a good

Illustration 15
Hand Action For Different Type Curve Balls

Illustration 15A
Area of Forearm That Must Face Batter For Good Curve Ball

pitch to use to force the batter to hit into a double play as it is usually hit into the ground. More will be said on when and where to throw the curve in the chapter on pitching strategy.

THE CHANGE-OF-PACE OFF THE CURVE BALL

The change off the curve can be thrown by turning the hand in at a maximum angle and holding the ball farther back in the fingers. If this does not produce a slow enough curve the principle of holding the foot back can be added. The pitcher must be careful to keep the change-up curve low as it has a tendency to hang more than the regular and extra curve.

REPERTORY OF CURVES

We have discussed the methods of changing the break and speed of the curve ball. The pitcher must be able to differentiate between his change-up curve, his regular curve and his extra curve. He must be able to push the button for the curve he needs. After learning the techniques of throwing the various pitches, real success lies in the pitcher's consistent ability to call upon these pitches when he needs them.

The pitcher shows his regular curve to the batter to set up his extra curve. The regular curve must not be considered as an easy curve but should be thought of as a good breaking curve, below the waist, thrown for a strike. The pitcher should be able to throw it with confidence on three and two and three and one counts.

The extra curve is used as a strike-out pitch. It should be thrown when the pitcher is ahead of the batter. As an illustration we will set up a hypothetical hitter. There is an important run in scoring position and a notoriously fast ball hitter at the plate. The first pitch is a regular curve below the waist taken for a strike. The next pitch is a high inside fast ball for a ball. With the count one and one the pitcher throws the regular curve low and away for a strike. The hitter has now seen two regular curves and is set up for the extra curve which the pitcher attempts to throw knee high or lower. The hitter is probably ready for a curve, but not ready to contend with the extra curve and he is not in a position to take anything close. The pitcher can afford to put something extra on this pitch and try to cut the knees because even if it is a ball he is still in a good position to work on the hitter. As we mentioned before the secret of the success of the extra curve depends upon the fact that it appears to be the regular curve but fools the batter with the extra action.

The pitcher now has the weapons to be a successful pitcher; our job is to aid him in pushing the right button at the right time and to make sure he is getting the desired result when he pushes each button.

♦ Specialty Pitches

seven

The pitcher's normal assortment of pitches consists of the fast ball, the curve, and the change-of-pace off these two pitches. When the pitcher is able to throw his fast ball and curve at several different speeds, this gives him a wide assortment of weapons with which to fool the batter.

Sometimes in a pitcher's career the need arises to supplement his basic repertory with a new pitch or pitches. These supplemental pitches can be variations of the basic offerings or, as often is the case, they can be entirely new pitches.

These specialty pitches are developed through copying others, experimenting, and adapting a pitch to one's individual physical characteristics and pitching needs. It usually takes several years of experimenting and adjusting to master one of these pitches.

CRITERIA FOR ADDING A SPECIALTY PITCH

The pitcher should not take on one of these pitches without carefully analyzing his strengths and weaknesses. He must have a definite reason for adding the pitch. First of all, the curve ball is needed along with the fast ball, to force the batter to deal with pitches breaking on different planes. By changing speeds on both the curve and fast ball the pitcher forces the batter not only to contend with the different planes but also with the variance in speed of the pitches. The pitcher who possesses a fast ball, a curve, and can change speeds on both these pitches has quite a repertory of weapons with which to fool the hitter. If they are working effectively, he need not spend his time trying to develop a freak pitch.

123

A pitcher with a mediocre fast ball who cannot throw a good curve ball may have to resort to a specialty pitch. It may be a pitch like the sinker or slider that comes up like a fast ball and breaks at the last minute, or an entirely different type pitch, such as the knuckle ball. The reason for adding a specialty pitch is to give the batter something else to think about in addition to the pitcher's otherwise mediocre weapons. The side-arm pitcher, for example, usually has trouble throwing the down-breaking curve and may find his style easily adaptable to throwing the sinker. The pitcher should not adopt a specialty pitch unless after careful analyzing he feels it is definitely needed in order for him to be effective.

CAUTIONS IN ADDING A SPECIALTY PITCH

Many of the pitchers who add a specialty pitch to their repertoire have pitched for many years and feel the need to add a new pitch because they are losing something off one of their basic pitches. They need the new pitch to keep the hitters honest. There are also a few pitchers in baseball that are relief specialists or spot specialists who only throw one pitch, such as the sinker or knuckle ball. These pitchers come into the game to make the batter hit the ball on the ground or to get important outs in a tight situation.

The young pitcher in the early stages of development does not fit under any of these categories. It is difficult enough for him to master control of his basic pitches. Some of the freak pitches may also do damage to his arm.

As has been mentioned throughout the book, learning to pitch depends to a large extent upon developing certain basic habits. The curve ball as described in chapter six is an example of this process. In learning the slider, described later in the chapter, a three-to-nine flat spin is imparted on the ball as opposed to the twelve-to-six rotation of the down-breaking curve.

We have seen many a young pitcher lose his good curve ball, by attempting to learn the slider before he is fully developed. To the hitter's delight, the pitch usually ends up halfway between a bad slider and a bad curve.

The question might well be asked, "If we make the recommendation that the young pitcher not attempt to learn the freak pitches, why include them in the book?" It may be that there are some pitchers in high school who need a specialty pitch with which to get by. The coach should be aware of the mechanics and use of the special pitches so that he will be better able to decide whether he should allow the pitcher to incorporate them into his repertory. If he does decide to incorporate a specialty pitch, he must know how to teach it and know how to fit it into the pitcher's basic pattern of pitching. In the majority of cases we recommend, however, that the young pitcher concentrate on the fast ball, curve, and change-of-pace. Leave the freak pitches to the old timers.

THE SLIDER

The slider is used by so many pitchers these days that it is no longer considered a specialty pitch. Many pitchers have added it to their regular repertoire of pitches. The slider breaks faster and flatter than the good curve. Its strength rests on the fact that it looks like a fast ball coming up to the batter and then breaks the last minute. The batter can usually pick up the curve ball's motion and spin sooner than that of the slider. The slider is not difficult to control and does not break as much as the curve. It usually rotates in a three-to-nine counter clockwise direction.

Use of the slider

The slider can be used successfully to keep the hitter off balance. It looks like a fast ball to the batter and then breaks away making it difficult for him to pull. The batter usually starts his swing expecting to pull what appears to be a fast ball, and then at the last minute the slider breaks away throwing the batter off balance.

The slider is usually easier to control than the big curve because it does not break as much. It could be used by the good fast ball pitcher as his percentage pitch. (See chapter nine.) The slider should be kept low and away to be effective. The exception might be when the pitcher is attempting to waste a pitch and jam an opposite side hitter (right handed pitcher against left handed hitter and vice-versa). The pitcher should grip the slider the same as he does his other pitches. In throwing the slider the pitcher attempts to get the button on the ball that is the mark of a poor curve ball.

Method of throwing the slider

The ball is thrown harder than the curve ball and resembles the action needed to make a football spiral.

Have the pitcher place the index and middle finger across the wide seams (if this is his natural fingering) with the thumb underneath the ball. Directions will be for the right handed pitcher and need only be reversed for the left hander. As the hand reaches about ear level it is rotated counter clockwise so that the thumb is now on the side of the ball nearest the pitcher's head and the index and middle fingers are on the opposite side of the ball. As the follow-through is completed the hand is rotated counter clockwise the ball being released off the side of the index finger. As a point of information, the part of the operation similar to throwing the football is the part where the thumb is on the head side of the ball with the hand going forward to throw. As the ball is released the hand is rotated further.

Dangers of the slider

The slider can be hard on the arm because of the strain involved at the elbow in the rotation. The trajectory of the slider is flatter than the curve and is easier to hit if it is not kept low and away. The most important disadvantage of teaching the slider is that it tends to detract from the young pitcher's curve ball. The major battle in teaching the curve is to get the pitcher to release the ball over the top of the fingers, rather than off the sides, as most young pitchers are prone to do. As you can see, the action of releasing the slider is getting away from the emphasis placed upon the pitcher in developing his curve. Unless the pitcher is very mature, learning the slider may interfere with the development of a good curve ball.

THE SCREW BALL

The screw ball, in essence, is a backwards curve. It breaks the opposite way from the curve. If the right handed pitcher throws it to a right handed batter it will break in on the batter. There have been several pitchers in the major leagues who have had good screw balls and have used them to good advantage.

Method of throwing the screw ball

The ball may be gripped in the normal manner. The pitcher attempts to impart a nine-to-three or clockwise spin on the ball. (Directions are for the right handed pitcher.) As the arm is brought forward the forearm is rotated clockwise or inward so that the index and middle fingers are on the pitcher's side of the ball during its release. The thumb plays a major role in imparting the clockwise rotation on the ball. Screw ball pitchers have been known to wear blisters on the top side of their thumbs because of the pressure exerted.

Dangers of the screw ball

The screw ball is a difficult pitch to master and is exceptionally hard on the young arm. The clockwise or inward rotation of the arm is unnatural and places undue strain on it.

ADDITIONAL BREAKING PITCHES

The remainder of the breaking pitches are classified under one heading because they all have something in common. The object of all these pitches is to make the ball move in an unnatural manner by exerting some type of uneven pressure on the ball, or by causing the ball to rotate unevenly against the atmosphere. Experienced pitchers have developed many unique ways of accomplishing these purposes. The principle of the emery ball, the spitter, the cut ball etc., were, or are, based on the same principle of uneven pressure. We will attempt in this section to describe some of the legal ways this principle is accomplished. As the pitcher becomes experienced he may want to experiment to find ways to make his ball move in different directions.

The sinker

The sinker is many times thrown by a side arm pitcher and is one of the greatest weapons of the relief artist. A good sinker forces the batter to hit the ball on the ground. It *must* be kept low or the action of the ball is not good. In throwing the sinker the pitcher turns the ball over, thus imparting a downward spin.

Method of throwing the sinker. The method of throwing the sinker resembles to some extent the method of throwing the screw ball. The main difference is that the emphasis is on the action and pressure of the index finger rather than on the inward rotation of the wrist. To get the idea of the sinker, hold the ball out away from you and slightly behind your right ear, with the index and middle fingers behind the ball and the thumb in front. Now, rotate the hand inward and downward so that you are looking at the back of your hand as the ball is literally turned over the thumb. It is important to exert pressure with the index finger as the ball is released. Spreading the fingers on the ball when attempting to throw the sinker often helps the action of the ball. Remember, the sinker must be kept low.

The knuckle ball

Of all the specialty pitches the knuckle ball is probably the most famous. Much publicity has been given this pitch because of the difficulty catchers have in catching it and the over sized gloves worn by some catchers when a knuckle baller is throwing. The knuckle ball takes probably the most erratic courses to the plate of any type pitch. It may sink, swerve to either side, or jump crazily. Its movement is highly unpredictable. These qualities also make it a difficult pitch for the pitcher to control. The knuckle ball barely rotates at all and seems to come up to the plate dead and then explodes one way or another.

Method of throwing the knuckle ball. There are several methods for throwing the knuckle ball. It can be thrown by digging the finger nails into the seams (some pitchers sharpen their finger nails for this) or by placing the first joints of the fingers on the ball. It can be thrown with one, two, or three fingers. Most pitchers use the two finger knuckle ball. The knuckle ball is thrown with a dead wrist similar to the change-of-pace, but it is thrown hard. The knuckle ball is difficult to control and usually takes years to develop. It is certainly not recommended for high school pitchers.

The fork ball

The fork ball is held between the index and middle fingers and is released with a vigorous wrist snap. A good fork ball comes up to the plate similar in action to the knuckle ball, and then the bottom seems to drop out of it, as it sinks. Several relief specialists have made this pitch famous. The young pitcher should not try to add this pitch to his repertoire.

Additional ideas on moving the ball

If the young pitcher has difficulty getting his ball to move he may do some experimenting paying attention to the uneven-pressure principle. He can get the ball to sail by placing the fingers on the smooth part of the ball and exerting pressure with the middle finger as he releases the ball. The ball can often be made to sink by using the same method and exerting pressure with the index finger. Gripping the ball off center, or on one seam, are other methods that can be employed to make the ball move.

There are many different ways to get a ball to move from its normal trajectory. We have presented some of these methods. When the pitcher has mastered his other pitches, and after careful self analysis feels he needs an additional pitch, he may consider these. But we do not recommend these specialty pitches for the young pitcher. The young pitcher will do well to master his fast ball and curve and the change of speeds off these pitches. Remember, he still must learn how, when, and where, to use these basic pitches to his greatest advantage.

◆ Control

eight

Our potentially successful pitcher is now equipped with the pitches he needs. But no matter how great these pitches are, they have little value if the pitcher cannot throw them where he wants. The pitcher must not only push the button and get the good breaking curve but the curve must go where he wants it to go. Many a great pitching prospect with good stuff has failed because of poor control, for without control, the pitcher deteriorates into a thrower, and finds himself always behind the hitter, and then having to throw the hitter's pitch. Throwers do not win! Pitching authorities regard good control as the most important feature of pitching. There are two sides to control, the physical and the mental, both are dealt with in detail here.

INGREDIENTS OF GOOD CONTROL

Good control is certainly the ability to throw strikes and keep the number of bases on balls to a minimum, but it does not end here. Strange as it may sound, good control is also the ability to throw balls. There are times in the pitching strategy when the pitcher wants to throw a ball to set up the next pitch or to keep the batter from hitting the ball. If this attempted ball sneaks into the strike zone it often spells disaster for the pitcher. As an example, there is an important run on second base with a good hitter at the plate. The next hitter is not as strong. The pitcher has a two and two count on the batter and wants to tempt him to go for a fast ball thrown for a ball off the plate. The pitcher does not want to throw the hitter anything fat because first base is open. His control is bad and the fast ball gets into the fat area, the hitter getting a base hit. Poor control and not being able to throw the pitch where he wanted for a ball cost the pitcher a run. Another case where a pitcher might be trying to throw a ball would be when he is showing the batter his regular curve, or fast ball, but does not want him to hit it, in order to set up his extra strikeout pitch on the next delivery. If this regular pitch gets in for a strike the hitter may hit it, which would defeat the pitcher's purpose.

The pitcher with good control is able to keep ahead in the count so that he can afford to set the hitter up and make him hit something he does not like. If the pitcher has poor control and he falls behind in the count, he must keep coming in with good strikes which the batter has a better chance of hitting.

Good control allows a pitcher to pitch to spots. By spots we mean trying to hit the corners and throwing to the batter's specific weakness. The pitcher with poor control must throw the ball down the pipe and hope his natural stuff takes care of the corners. There is no use talking about pitching in and out, high and low, or everything low if the pitcher does not have the control to do so. The successful pitcher has the ability to throw to spots.

Many coaches like to move their outfielders and infielders around to where they think each hitter is most likely to hit the ball. This is fine and certainly is playing the percentages, *if* your pitcher has the control to pitch accordingly. If you have shifted your outfield around because the hitter is an opposite field hitter and your pitcher gets a slow curve inside instead of outside, you are in trouble, as the hitter will pull this pitch and cross up your defense. The pitcher is the key to the defense and must have good control to make it work.

Control in all conditions

The successful pitcher must be consistent and have good control under all conditions. He must be able to pitch with control under pressure. There are defensive situations where the pitcher can help his team by being able to pitch to certain spots. We have listed some of these to illustrate the important part the control pitcher plays in the team defense.

1. Double play situation. Keep the ball low and preferably throw a down breaking pitch trying to make the batter hit the ball on the ground.

2. Important runner on second, no outs. Try to keep the ball high and tight to keep the right handed hitter from hitting a ground ball to the opposite side of the infield, moving the runner to third.

3. Same situation, left handed hitter. Try to keep him from pulling ground ball, by pitching him outside.

4. Bunt situation. Throw him high and hard.

5. Squeeze play. Throw him inside for right handed batter and outside for left handed batter.

6. Man on third, none or one out. Must pitch low to keep batter from hitting scoring fly ball. Must also keep him from hitting a ground ball to the right side.

There are other situations in which the pitcher is called upon to pitch to certain spots for defensive purposes, but the preceding will serve to illustrate the importance of good control. In any of these situations, a poorly placed pitch could ruin the defense. Of course in all these situations the type hitter, the philosophy of the offensive team, and the score must be considered.

THE PHYSICAL SIDE OF CONTROL

The pitcher must be consistent in his form to have good control. He must strive as nearly as possible to deliver each pitch in the same way. If he is consistent about this, it will be possible for him to adjust when he is wild. We call this our zeroing in process, like that of a rifleman who zeros in his sights on the target. If he is shooting consistently high, he lowers his sights;

consistently to the left he adjusts to the right. If the rifleman is not holding his rifle true, or holds it at his shoulder one time, and at his waist another time, he will not be able to zero in. His actions must be consistent in order to adjust the sights. The same is true of a pitcher. If his pitching motion is the same on each pitch and he is consistently high he can adjust, but if he throws one pitch over-hand, one side-arm, one from the right of the rubber, and one from the left, the adjustment is impossible to make. Consistency of delivery is the secret.

Causes of poor control

Physically, poor control is usually caused by some "flaw" in the delivery which *can be corrected*. We have discussed at length, proper form and delivery for each pitch but to aid you in helping the wild pitcher, the basic causes of wildness are discussed on the following pages.

Taking the eyes off the target. The eyes must remain constantly on the target throughout the delivery. Some pitchers lose sight of the target by dipping their head and looking toward the ground in the middle of their delivery. Others lose the target by tucking their head behind the shoulder when they are in the lay-back position. A combination of these two faults is the pitcher who jerks his head when he throws, usually in an attempt to throw the ball harder. With men on base, the pitcher must remember to fix his eyes back on the target before going to the plate. The pitcher must fix his gaze upon the target and *concentrate*. He should pause and ask himself, what, where, how, and why, he is throwing that particular pitch. Have him practice without moving his head. Allow him to pitch only as hard as he can, *without* moving his head. It may take a little prodding on your part to force the pitcher to keep his eyes on the target.

Landing on his heel. When the pitcher strides he should not land on his heel. If he does it jars his whole body and throws his control off. The stride should be made on the ball of the foot.

Throwing across the body. When a pitcher throws across his body he locks his hips and it impedes the smooth delivery and follow through. To avoid this, have him open his hips by striding across the center line. The stride foot should at least be placed on the center line and more preferably to the left of it. The pitcher should be warned about striding too far to the left of the center line as this will tend to dissipate his power. (For right handed pitchers.)

Varying the arm angle. The pitcher who varies his arm angle has little chance of having good control. As we mentioned before, some experienced pitchers do vary the arm angle on different pitches but this is not recommended for young pitchers. Every pitch should be thrown from the same angle so that the pitcher learns to feel his groove and can also adjust (zeroing in principle) when he is consistently wild in one direction or another.

Moving around on the rubber. Contrary to some beliefs, we feel that moving around on the rubber hurts control more than it helps it. The pitcher should become accustomed to pitching from the same spot on the rubber on each pitch. We prefer to have our right handers pick a spot to the right of the center of the rubber and vice-versa for our left handers. If the pitcher always pitchers from the same spot he can better "zero" in and adjust.

Over- and under-striding. Over- or under-striding can cause control problems. The stride should be de-emphasized. Too many pitchers concentrate too much on the length of their stride. The pitcher should *stride to throw*, the stride being only a *part* of the process. We illustrate this to our pitchers by standing about two feet in front of them and telling them to *pretend* they are going to hit us with their pitching hand. They step toward us to do this but they are not conscious of emphasizing the stride, which is what we want.

Poor physical condition. The pitcher who is in poor physical condition is going to have control problems. Physical conditioning was discussed in chapter three but its importance concerning the pitcher's control cannot be over-emphasized. The pitcher has enough problems without having to worry about being off because he is not in shape. We illustrate the importance of the pitcher's legs being in shape by having him run until his legs are shaky and then asking him to pitch. The pitcher will readily understand the problems involved if his under-pinning is shaky. We do this *once* for illustrative purposes only, we do not recommend it for anything else. Body flexibility is also important if the pitcher is to maintain excellent control. This means stretching exercises everyday as recommended in chapter three. The pitcher who is stiff and inflexible cannot hope to achieve good control. The pitcher must also have the stamina to remain steady and strong over a nine inning period or his control will suffer as he grows weary.

Excessive movement. Some pitchers put so much effort into their wind-up and preliminary actions that their control is hindered. Try to cut down on this by helping the pitcher develop a smooth, efficient, delivery. We have aided pitchers of this type by changing their delivery to the no-wind-up style. If you have an exceptionally wild pitcher who has an exaggerated action try the no-wind-up approach. Have him hold the ball in the glove in front of him at the belt buckle, take a deep breath and then deliver the ball.

Uneven finger pressure. Many times the cause of wildness is uneven finger pressure on the ball. This is also the cause of a good live ball which we all like to see in our pitchers. There are a few cases where certain pitchers never did achieve control because of a tremendous amount of uneven pressure exerted by the fingers. These cases are the exception rather than the rule. If you are blessed with a pitcher who has an exceptionally live ball, but hard to control, have him throw it down the middle of the strike zone and allow the liveness to take care of the corners.

Aiming the ball. Aiming the ball is one of the most common causes of poor control, especially the momentary loss of control. The well coached pitcher has worked hard and long on his form and smooth, efficient, delivery of the ball. When he aims the ball he is discarding all that he has attained and is going back to *throwing* the ball. This usually happens in a tight situation when the pressure is on. It should be pointed out to the pitcher that his form and delivery are sound and they will serve him well in the pressure spots just as they do when the pressure is off. He should not change his whole technique because he is in a tight spot, but must rely on what he has learned and developed to get him out of the spot. The pitcher *must* believe in this if he is going to be successful.

Wild from the stretch. Being wild from the stretch position with men on base is usually caused by inexperience in dealing with the situation. Coaches often times neglect having their pitchers practice from this position. Beginning pitchers should spend close to half their practice time pitching from the stretch position.

Aids to good control

To help your pitchers in achieving good control, we list some of the major points to be stressed:

1. The pitcher should keep his eyes on the target throughout the delivery.
2. The pitcher should grip all the pitches in the same manner.
3. The stride should be made on the ball of the foot, to the left

of the center line with the foot pointed toward the target. (Right handed pitchers.)
4. The pitcher should find *his* point of release, and release the ball well out in front each time.
5. The pitcher should never throw a ball unless he is throwing over a plate. (We make him bring a wooden plate with him and use it whenever he throws.)
6. The pitcher should throw through the strings during practice.
7. The pitcher should avoid excessive movement in his delivery.
8. The pitcher must avoid aiming the ball.
9. The pitcher should throw from the same arm angle on each pitch.
10. The pitcher should throw from the same spot on the rubber on each pitch.
11. The pitcher should spend time practicing from the stretch position.
12. The pitcher should not over-emphasize his stride.
13. The pitcher must keep himself in top physical condition.
14. The pitcher should practice good form and delivery until he pitches smoothly from *habit*.
15. The pitcher must adjust to different size mounds.

The coach must constantly check the pitcher's form and delivery for flaws that might be the cause of poor control. The various drills mentioned to improve form and the delivery of the specific pitches should be repeated from time to time to strengthen the good pitching habits (see chapter twelve).

THE MENTAL SIDE OF CONTROL

Mental attitude usually has more influence upon control than do physical flaws. The physical flaws can be easily observed, diagnosed, and corrected while mental problems are much harder to remedy.

If the successful environment has been carefully developed and the relationship between you and the pitcher is one of mutual confidence, mental problems will be at a minimum. Problems such as aiming the ball, choking, and getting the "olive" are all problems of the mind. These problems are brought to the forefront in pressure situations when fine control is needed. In chapter one, we discussed at great length, building the successful environment, building confidence, and dealing with fear. It might be beneficial to refer to these sections at this time. In this section we shall be dealing specifically with how to aid control and meet mental problems.

Mental reasons for wildness

Before discussing the methods of combating mental wildness, we should like to present the negative side of the problem by listing some of the causes of mental wildness.

1. Fear of failure.
2. Unfamiliarity with the situation at hand.
3. Distracting influence of the crowd and the noise.
4. The "Ty Cobb" type base runner.
5. "Rabbit Ears."
6. Lack of concentration on the job at hand.
7. Lack of push-button confidence in his pitches.
8. Lack of confidence exhibited by his teammates.

Fighting fear with knowledge

The major reason a pitcher is fearful in a tight situation is that he does not know how to cope with the situation. An old pro looks confident under pressure because he has the *knowledge* to know what to do and has met the situation before. It is your responsibility to see that the pitcher knows what to do in these tight situations. A well prepared pitcher is *not* fearful.

Practice aids to confidence. It is not enough to merely *talk* about fighting fear with knowledge, it must actually be done in practice. The pitcher should practice under pressure meeting all the situations that might come up in a game. Pressure should be put on the pitcher everyday. The pitcher should be trained in practice to concentrate on *positive* actions.

To help you set up in practice the pressure situations that might occur in the game, a list of drills and exercises are presented with a brief description of their content. The actual procedures for the drills are presented in chapter twelve. Drills on fielding which are very important in aiding the pitcher's confidence and thus his control are discussed in chapter ten.

1. Ten-minute daily pressure drill through the strings. The pitcher puts pressure on himself by simulating pitching to actual hitters under game situations while throwing through the strings for control.

2. The live stopper drill. The pitcher is called in to meet three and two, bases loaded situations, and the like, and only gets one chance to put out the fire.

3. The game situation drill. The pitcher faces the batters under actual game situations and may pitch for a certain number of outs.

4. The coach's pressure drill. While the pitcher is engaged in regular practice throwing to the catcher, the coach comes up behind him and sets up a hypothetical pressure situation on the spur of the moment.

5. Assumed pressure drill before the game and between innings. The pitcher sets up hitters and imagines hypothetical pressure situations when finishing his warmups.

The success of these drills lies in your ability to make them as realistic as possible and to thoroughly explain how to meet each situation. You must have the pitcher tackle each situation over and over until it becomes second nature to him. If the pitcher faces the various situations many times he will develop confidence in his ability to deal with them and he will be able to push the right button at the right time. Do not expect any pitcher to meet a situation expertly that he has never before experienced.

Some thoughts on pressure

Without pressure, victory would not be as sweet. What thrill winning the World Series if no crowd was present, no money or prestige was attached and thus no pressure to overcome? Pressure must be looked upon as the opportunity to prove oneself, not as something to be feared. Poise and confidence, the major combatives of mental pressure, are gained through much practice and experience. If the pitcher is aware of what to do and has done it many times, the pressure of the moment will not hurt his control and he will be able to adjust to the pressure situation. You should take time to sit down with your pitchers and discuss the problems of pressure and the philosophy of dealing with them. Do not *ignore* pressure, explore it and handle it! Nine times out of ten if your pitcher chokes, it is your fault. It is your responsibility to explain the unknown, to impart knowledge, and to instill confidence in your pitchers.

The coach and confidence

You have much to do with the amount of confidence your pitching staff possesses. You must be *sensitive* to your pitcher's needs and treat him with candor when it comes to criticizing him or taking him out of the ball game.

How to remove a pitcher. There comes a day in every pitcher's life when he has to be relieved. The way you handle taking him out will have much to do with his future confidence. Be considerate and do not embarrass the pitcher by bawling him out in front of the crowd. This is not the time to teach him how to pitch, either. Go out briskly, bring in your relief man, give your starter a pat on the back and get out of there. Do not make a career out of relieving your pitcher. Do the masterminding in the dugout. When you go to the mound, go for a purpose.

When to remove a pitcher. One of the responsibilities of coaching baseball is to make the decision as to when a pitcher has had enough. You must consider the caliber of the opposition, the caliber of your relief man, the score, the runners, and the type batter, and then you must make your decision. Good luck!

We are more concerned here with the effect relieving the pitcher has upon his confidence and control. Leaving the pitcher in and relieving him at the right time can have a tremendous effect upon his confidence. For the sake of making our point, let us assume that we are talking about practice games in which we are trying to build our pitching staff's confidence. We are concerned with the opportune time to take the pitcher out. If you are trying to help the pitcher's control, it is a good idea to take him out if he has had a good inning or two, rather than wait and face the possibility of his confidence going down the drain with a bad inning. On the other hand, if the going is a little shaky, let him pitch and give him a chance to work his way out of trouble. You may need him later in the season. Do not, however, let him get beat to death.

Follow-up techniques. When you have jerked your pitcher and given him the pat on the back let him alone. Give him a chance to gather himself together before you begin telling him what was wrong. We keep detailed charts on our pitchers and when they have left the game they pick these up and go over them. We feel one of the greatest strengths of these charts is that they afford the pitcher an opportunity to objectively go over his performance without the coach irritating him with his gifted words at this delicate time. When the game is over, each pitcher comes to the office and picks up his pitcher's summary sheets, discusses his performance with us, and then takes the forms home and fills them out. During this cooling-off period after the game, we try to constructively build the pitcher's confidence by discussing his strengths and weaknesses and how he can improve his performance. Point out the places where his control was good. You must always strive to end your discussion with a positive comment to stimulate the pitcher to do better next time and to allow him to leave your office encouraged rather than discouraged.

The catcher

The catcher plays an important part in aiding the pitcher's control and confidence. It has often been said, "A great catcher can make a great pitcher out of a mediocre one." As this is a book on pitching, we only list briefly some of the ways the catcher can help aid the pitcher's control.

1. Give a steady target. Give the signal and get set, so that the pitcher will not be distracted by having to pitch to a moving target.
2. Receive the pitch with the arms and hands out in front, catching the ball close to the plate to give the umpire a better view of the strike. Catch the ball while it is a strike.
3. Do not pull pitches into the strike zone that are ridiculous; we will be satisfied if we get the borderline calls. Remember, we are not trying to fool the umpire but are trying to get the calls that *are* strikes.
4. Keep low, with the hips above the knees, and the glove low.
5. Do not bob up and down obstructing the umpire's view.
6. Receive the ball with the catching hand at a right angle to the ground (hand pointing either straight up or straight down).
7. Return the ball to the pitcher accurately, do not irritate him and tire him needlessly by making him field your bad throws.
8. Know your pitcher, his strengths and his weaknesses, and be able to set up his pitching pattern accordingly.

We treat our catchers as pitchers in the early stages of their development. We insist that they learn the fundamentals of pitching right along with our pitchers. They learn how to spin the curve, throw the change, adjust to poor rotation, etc., as if they were pitchers. If they have this background they will better be able to observe and help the pitcher when he is in trouble. A sensitive catcher, if he has the knowledge, should detect the reason for the pitcher's ineffectiveness sooner than the coach or the pitcher himself. By keeping a close check on the pitcher's development, the catcher can better aid him. The catcher must also be sensitive to the pitcher's disposition so that he does not irritate him. Some pitchers are better left alone during the game and some require constant leadership and direction from the catcher. It is the catcher's job to treat each pitcher according to each pitcher's needs. When we hear one of our pitchers in practice asking the catcher if the curve ball is breaking into the ground because he is cutting through the barrel, we know the relationship we want is developing.

The team

There is nothing that hurts a pitcher's control more than to have his infielders gripe, "For crying out loud, get the ball in there!" The pitcher has enough trouble without having his own teammates on his back. As mentioned in an earlier chapter, the situation can also be reversed if the pitcher throws his glove down in disgust when a teammate makes an error. A team with this attitude *will not* win! Each member of the team must be ready to encourage the other when he is in trouble. The pitcher especially needs this support when he is wild.

Concentration

One of the greatest attributes that any successful performer possesses is the power of concentration. If the pitcher is concentrating positively on how to get the batter out, he will not have time to worry about failure, about the crowd, or about what the opposition is yelling at him.

We make it a rule for our pitcher never to throw a pitch unless there is a reason for it. If they do not know what, where, how, and why they are throwing the pitch they should not throw it. In practice make it a habit to stop your pitcher from time to time and ask him these questions. If he does not have the answers, he is not concentrating. If he is not concentrating, he is not pitching, and if he is not pitching, he *will not win*.

To aid the pitcher who works too fast and does not think, have him stop, take a deep breath, and ask himself what, where, how, and why. Demand that he answer these questions to himself before delivering each pitch and it will help his concentration.

Good control is not easily learned nor is it always present, but the pitcher who adheres to sound basic fundamentals and has confidence in his push-button system is well on his way to having consistently fine control.

◆ Pitching Strategy

nine

Pitching strategy must be taught as methodically and scientifically as the teaching of the curve or any other phase of the pitcher's development. It is no accident that some pitchers are described as "pitchers that know how to pitch" or "pitchers that know how to set up the hitters." This skill of learning to use the head as well as the arm in pitching successfully can and must be developed. In this chapter we shall endeavor to take the guess work out of pitching strategy and present an organized plan for the development of your pitcher's formula for getting the hitter out.

IMPORTANCE OF A SHARP-THINKING PITCHER

As mentioned previously there are few pitchers that can throw the ball by the hitters consistently. Conversely, there are many pitchers that do not throw hard that get the hitters out consistently by using their heads. The thinking pitcher relies upon his ability to pitch to the hitter's weakness, and to set up the batter to hit the pitch he wants him to hit. Many hard throwers, even in the major leagues, have learned the hard way that they have to think and mix up their pitches *intelligently* in order to be successful.

MINIMUM SKILLS NEEDED BY THE THINKING PITCHER

There is no use talking about pitching strategy and outthinking the batter unless the pitcher possesses the minimum weapons to put his plan into effect. He should be able to push the button and get the pitch he wants. We have discussed in previous chap-

147

ters, the development of the weapons needed by the successful pitcher. We realize that each pitcher's assortment of weapons will vary, but we feel there is a basic minimum assortment of pitches that all pitchers should strive to acquire. All of these pitches have been discussed previously so we will merely list them for reference at this time.

1. The 90% fast ball and the 98% fast ball.
2. The regular curve and the extra curve.
3. The change-of-pace off the fast ball.
4. The change-of-pace off the curve ball.
5. Fine control of the pitches acquired.

The pitcher is now at the stage of learning how to efficiently use the weapons he has acquired. Just as a random selection of different colored paints does not make the picture, a random selection of curve balls, fast balls, and changes does not make the pitcher.

SELF-ANALYSIS BY THE PITCHER

The coach must help the pitcher in analyzing himself. It must be determined whether he is a control pitcher, a predominately curve ball pitcher, a predominately fast ball pitcher, a pitcher that relies on changing speeds, or a pitcher that relies upon a combination of the preceding. Again, we point out, the pitcher must know himself.

By determining which pitch performs the best, i.e., an exceptionally live fast ball or a sharp breaking curve, and then determining which pitch can be thrown consistently where he wants it, the pitcher can learn which is his best pitch. After determining his strength or best pitch, he should analyze his weakness. Which is his weakest pitch, in terms of control and performance?

After analyzing his strengths and weaknesses he should fit each pitch into his pattern. Below are presented some questions to help in setting up the pitcher's general pattern of pitches.

1. Is his control such that he can throw any pitch on three and two, three and one, and two and nothing counts; or does he have to rely on one pitch in these cases?

2. Can he throw his secondary pitch for a strike when ahead in the count without doing the batter a favor?

3. Does he use his secondary pitch only to show the batter another pitch, or can it be relied upon to get the batter out?

4. Is his control such that he can afford to waste a pitch when he is ahead in order to set up the batter?

5. Does his best pitch rely upon the element of surprise or change of speeds to be effective, or does it perform so well that it is effective in and of itself?

6. Which pitch is his most effective strikeout pitch?

7. Which pitch is hit on the ground the most?

8. Which pitch is most likely to be hit in the air the most?

When the pitcher has analyzed his strengths and weaknesses and knows which pitch is most likely to do what, in a given situation, he is ready to start analyzing the hitter. It does the pitcher no good to know the hitter's strengths, weaknesses, and idiosyncrasies if he does not know his own.

ANALYZING AND PITCHING TO DIFFERENT KINDS OF HITTERS

Analyzing the batter is not a hit or miss proposition. To aid you and your pitcher to systematically analyze the hitters we will present many of the common characteristics to look for and also will recommend the most accepted way to pitch to each type hitter.

The coach must be cautioned that the following tendencies and remedies are only generalities. They are presented with the purpose of demonstrating how batters may be classified and how, *in general*, certain type hitters may best be pitched.

Carefully observing the opposing hitters, classifying them,

and pitching accordingly is much better than pitching to them in blind ignorance. The classifications presented and remedies suggested are only clues toward pitching successfully to each hitter. Remember, the pitcher should first analyze himself and then analyze the hitter. After pitching the hitter a certain way the pitcher should make notes on the effectiveness of the method and then adjust accordingly. The suggestions we make are only initial steps and should be looked upon as a very rough estimate of how to pitch each hitter. It should also be noted that many of the classifications presented overlap and that some hitters possess a combination of characteristics.

Mental characteristics

Each hitter has his own hitting personality. We classify them as the nervous or anxious hitter, the lazy hitter, the confident hitter, and the guesser or thinker. Each one of these hitters should be pitched to differently.

Nervous or anxious hitter. This type hitter is fidgety at the plate and anxious to get going. He is often a first ball swinger. The pitcher should make him wait, and even double or triple pump him to add to his anxiety. Often this type hitter can be teased into swinging at bad balls.

Lazy hitter. The lazy hitter likes to take his time at the plate and does not like to be rushed. The pitcher should work faster on this type hitter, forcing the hitter to perform according to the pitcher's rate of speed rather than this own. Often the fast ball can be buzzed past this type hitter on the first pitch.

Confident hitter. The confident hitter is, of course, the most difficult to contend with. The confident hitter is very choosy and knows what pitch he wants to hit. It is a good plan when dealing with this type hitter to throw pitches he does not like for strikes, thus getting ahead of him and forcing him to hit *your* pitch.

Guesser or thinker. Pitching to the guesser or thinker is a real battle of brains. This type hitter is trying to anticipate what the pitcher will throw. (Most hitters do this from time to time.) The pitcher in this case should try to think as if he were the hitter. If he is thinking *with* the hitter he has a good chance of fooling him.

Types of hitters

Each hitter has a peculiar physical style of hitting. It is our purpose in this section to present many of these different styles and recommend methods of pitching to them.

In analyzing the different type hitters it is very important to analyze his plate coverage. As an example, the choke hitter who stands close to the plate should be pitched differently from the choke hitter who stands away from the plate. Remember, when using the classifications and remedies we suggest, the batter's stance in relation to the plate should be your first consideration.

Whether the batter has a closed stance, an open stance or straight-away stance, a clue as to how to pitch him can be ascertained by watching his stride foot. If he strides in toward the plate he should be pitched inside and if he strides away he should be pitched outside.

Choke hitter. Most choke hitters choke up on the bat to help their hand action and bat control. They are the toughest kind of hitters to pitch to. They are hard to fool by change of speeds and it is also difficult to get the ball by them. The best plan is to work them in and out and try to jam them on the hands.

End gripper. The end gripper is usually a pull hitter and should be pitched away. They have poorer bat control than the choke hitters and changing speeds often throws them off balance.

Free swinger. The free swinger is usually going for the long ball and thus gives up an amount of bat control. He should be given off-speed pitches and breaking pitches to catch him off balance. This type hitter commits himself early and finds it difficult to hold up on changes and breaking pitches.

Thick handle swinger. The thick handle swinger usually likes to poke the ball to all fields and likes pitches away, and often likes breaking pitches. Throw him hard and tight.

Thin handle swinger. The thin handle swinger usually is trying to pull the ball and should be pitched away.

Lazy wrist hitter. The lazy wrist hitter is oftentimes slow getting around on the ball and should be pitched fast balls, inside. This type hitter often hits the off speed and breaking pitches well.

Long stride hitter. The long stride hitter can usually be thrown off balance by change-ups and breaking pitches as he does not have good body control and commits himself early.

Bat high hitter. When the bat is held straight up, the hitter may have a difficult time hitting the high hard fast ball. He usually is a low ball hitter and likes to golf the ball.

Flat bat hitter. The flat bat hitter usually hits the pitch around the eyes best; keep the ball low.

Crouch hitter. The crouch hitter should be pitched high as he is usually a low ball hitter.

Stand-up hitter. The straight up hitter should be pitched low.

Back shoulder dipper. This type hitter is an upper-cutter and will have trouble with the high pitch.

SOURCES OF INFORMATION ON BATTERS

The observation of opposing batters must be organized. The hitters must be observed as often as possible to get a complete rundown on them. As each particular situation varies, several different alternatives are presented. You may be able to use all or some of the suggestions in your specific situation.

Batting practice

If batting practice is allowed in your situation it can be an invaluable period to evaluate opposing hitters. Mimeographed forms should be used for ease of recording the information. The starting pitcher and several relief pitchers should do the observing with the aid of the coaches. The hitters should be classified and possible methods of pitching to them should be noted. It should also be noted where they seem to hit the ball the majority of the time.

Scouting procedures

There is usually someone in your school who will be happy to scout your opponents. You can often use some of your exball players, injured players, or assistant coaches. We recommend a special form for this report and the scout should pay particular attention to the type pitcher that the hitter is hitting against. The two charts, our subjective rating chart and our objective rating chart, should give a good indication of how best to pitch each hitter. A thorough explanation of how to use the charts is presented in chapter eleven. The opposing hitters can also be scouted in the summer baseball program.

Book on the batter

Each time a pitcher pitches to a batter the results should be recorded. The pitching chart explained in chapter eleven is ideal for this purpose. The pitcher must not only go over the results but must make note of *how* he pitches each hitter and make any adjustments that are necessary the next time he faces him.

A pitcher who is not pitching this particular day is responsible for keeping the charts and the pitcher in the game can refer to them between innings. The game pitcher is responsible for picking the charts up after the game, discussing them briefly with the coach, and then taking them home overnight. At home the pitcher summarizes the data, draws his conclusions, and is ready to go over them with the coach before school in the morning. (The use of the charts is discussed more thoroughly in chapter eleven.)

KEEPING THE HITTER OFF BALANCE

Keeping the hitter off balance is the secret to successful pitching. The hitter who is kept off balance never seems to get his pitch, never seems to hit the ball on the nose, and usually comes back to the bench muttering, "That guy doesn't look that impressive; I can't figure out why I don't hit him." Basically, there are four major methods of keeping the hitter off balance: (1) the pitcher's actions, (2) changing speeds on the ball, (3) changing the position of the ball, and (4) outthinking the hitter. They all overlap and may be interchangeable but for the sake of clarity they will each be presented separately.

Pitcher's actions

Each hitter has his own particular hitting rhythm. The effective pitcher should attempt to disrupt this rhythm, thereby keeping the hitter off balance.

Pitchers sometimes fall into the habit of pitching from the same rhythm all the time. Smart hitters learn to hit off the pitcher's rhythm. The pitcher must vary his pitching rhythm so that the batter cannot do this.

Varying the pumps. The pitcher can change his rhythm by varying his pumps, sometimes single pumping, sometimes double pumping, and from time to time triple pumping before delivering the pitch.

No wind-up. Many pitchers use the no wind-up approach to vary their rhythm. In the no wind-up method the pitcher can make the batter wait or can upset his timing by hurrying him.

Varying the time between pitches. This is one of the easiest methods to change rhythms. The pitcher merely changes the time intervals between the delivery of each pitch.

Shaking the sign off. The pitcher can often upset the batter by shaking the sign off several times even if it means returning to the original call. This not only makes the batter wait but it gets him thinking about what the pitcher *might* throw him. The pitcher should nod his head confidently when ready to pitch to further worry the hitter. It is a good device to use to keep the batter off balance.

The object of these methods is to pitch to the batter when he is not at his optimum moment of readiness and to prevent the batter from hitting off the pitcher's constant rhythm.

Changing speeds on the ball

The hitter can be kept off balance by changing speeds on the ball. If each type pitch is thrown constantly at the same speed the hitter will soon adjust to it and hit it. If the pitcher throws each type pitch at varying speeds, even the hitter that anticipates which pitch is coming still must contend with the variance in speed of the pitch.

A hypothetical case may further explain our idea. The batter is predominately a fast ball hitter. The count is two and two and he takes a regular curve for ball three. He knows the pitcher is a good curve ball pitcher and he anticipates the curve on three and two. He gets his curve but it is an extra curve and he is thrown off balance by the difference between the two curves. This is one of the reasons the successful pitcher must be able to throw his fast ball and curve at different speeds. The change-of-pace off the fast ball and curve, in addition to the regular and extra pitches, gives the pitcher three speeds for each type pitch.

Changing the position of the ball

The hitter can be further thrown off balance by "moving the ball around." A batter who is kept off balance in this way might be likened to a cork bobbing in the water, he never is quite stable or set on firm ground.

In and out. Many pitchers use the in and out method of keeping the batter off balance. The batter is moved back with an inside pitch and then thrown outside while he is on his heels. By constantly moving the ball inside and outside the hitter is not able to get set.

Up and down. The up and down principle can be used in nearly the same manner as the in and out method, although we recommend it be used in conjunction *with* the in and out plan of pitching.

Outthinking the hitter

Outthinking the hitter is actually a combination of the above methods of keeping the hitter off balance. In essence, the pitcher tries to throw the pitch that the batter leasts expects, at varying speeds, and in varying spots. The secret is for the pitcher to know himself, know the hitter, think with the hitter, and be able to push the button for the right pitch after considering the basic principles of successful pitching.

RULE PITCHING: A SIMPLE PLAN

Any successful plan of attack must be organized. This is true in war, business, athletics, and certainly is true in pitching. For an organized plan to be successful it must be well defined and the rules of operation clearly stated. It is much easier for the young pitcher to be able to follow simple rules for pitching strategy than it is for him to make random decisions based on vague generalizations.

In setting up our rules for pitching strategy we classify each ball and strike situation under one of four categories. These are termed the vulnerable situation, the percentage situation, the fine situation, and the extra fine situation.

Vulnerable situation

In the vulnerable situation the pitcher *must* get the ball in there for a strike. This situation occurs on three balls and two strikes, three balls and one strike, three balls and no strikes, and two balls and no strikes. The pitcher should strive to keep away from these counts which give the batter a decided advantage. For, if the pitcher throws a ball, the batter walks or, in the case of the two and nothing count, reaches three and nothing.

The pitcher must develop a pitch that he can get over for a strike in these situations with at least a "little something on it." The pitcher must not be so weak in this position that he must throw the ball up there to be hit.

Percentage situation

In the percentage situation the pitcher is trying to even the count or to keep from throwing a ball and thus get himself in the vulnerable position. The percentage situation occurs on the first pitch, one ball and no strikes, two balls and one strike, and two balls and two strike counts. In this situation the pitcher might throw a good change or regular curve trying to get the batter to hit the ball on the ground. The pitcher has done a good job in the percentage situation if he gets the batter to hit his pitch for an out.

Fine situation

The pitcher has a definite advantage in the fine situation. The fine situation occurs on no balls and one strike, one ball and one strike, and on one ball and two strikes. The pitcher can put something extra on the pitch without fear of it being a ball, as a ball will change the count to a percentage situation on the next pitch. This is a good spot to try to get the batter to hit a bad pitch or, with two strikes, to strike him out with an extra pitch.

Extra fine situation

This situation only occurs with a no balls and two strikes count. The pitcher should be trying to get the batter to swing at a bad pitch. He *should not* allow him to hit the ball. If the batter takes the pitch for a ball the pitcher is still in a fine position. How many times have you seen a hitter break up a ball game with a clean hit when in a nothing and two situation? There is no excuse for this, if the pitcher is thinking.

Over-view

In essence the plan is one of looking ahead to the next pitch and determining which situation the pitcher wants to be in. He should always be striving to be in the fine or extra fine positions. The vulnerable pitch is actually "Custer's last stand" and the percentage pitch is the one used to keep out of the vulnerable position, or to get into the fine position. To further clarify our underlying principle for setting up the pitcher's strategy the various counts are listed below with their classification following.

1. First pitch (percentage)
2. No balls—one strike (fine)
3. One ball—no strikes (percentage)
4. No balls—two strikes (extra fine)
5. Two balls—no strikes (vulnerable)
6. One ball—one strike (fine)
7. Three balls—no strikes (vulnerable)
8. One ball—two strikes (fine)
9. Two balls—one strike (percentage)
10. Three balls—one strike (vulnerable)
11. Two balls—two strikes (percentage)
12. Three balls—two strikes (vulnerable)

Illustrative example

To illustrate our plan, a hypothetical situation is set up. (This situation is structured to show how a pattern of pitches changes with the different counts.) There are no men on in the third inning, no score, two outs, and the fifth hitter is up. The batter was observed in batting practice; he uses a thin handled bat, holds it straight up, and appears to be a free swinger who strides away from the plate, definitely trying to pull the ball.

The pitcher has good control, can throw his fast ball and curve at varying speeds but is not overpowering.

First pitch. The pitcher, pitching the batter percentage, throws a curve for a called strike.

Second pitch. He is now in a fine situation, no balls and one strike. Attempting to pitch the batter fine, the pitcher misses with a fast ball outside.

Third pitch. He is still in an advantageous fine situation. The count is one ball and one strike. He throws his extra fast ball high and tight, which the batter misses for strike two.

Fourth pitch. He remains in the fine position and attempts to strike the batter out with an extra curve, low and outside. The batter takes the pitch for a ball.

Fifth pitch. With the count two balls and two strikes he is back in the percentage position. He wants the batter to hit the ball and throws a change-up off the curve on which the batter grounds out.

If this last pitch would have been a ball making the count three balls and two strikes you could see the total progression from percentage to fine to vulnerable. Study this illustration, the method is simple. It is a matter of applying a few rules before delivering each pitch. The system is organized and gives the pitcher something definite on which to base his strategy. The pitcher should not attempt to memorize the rules but should gain a practical knowledge of them so he can easily make use of them in the heat of battle.

VARIATIONS IN THE PLAN

The method prescribed on the preceding pages is flexible enough to be adjusted to meet varying situations. In most cases the plan can be followed as one would follow a specific formula. The variables and adjustments that can be made are explained on the following pages.

Type pitcher

If the pitcher has poor control some of the fine pitches may have to be moved to the percentage category. If his control is so bad that he cannot operate under this adjustment he is a thrower, not a pitcher.

If the pitcher, on the other hand, has exceptionally good control some of the percentage pitches can be moved to the fine category. The advantages and disadvantages of control pitching can be seen in this plan. The greater the number of fine and extra fine situations the greater the success of the pitcher. Some pitchers may pitch fine with their best pitch and will have to pitch percentage with their second pitch. These variables are not difficult to deal with if the coach and pitcher follow the prescribed methods for analyzing the pitcher.

Type batter

There are certain batters that the pitcher might pitch fine all the way because of their tremendous offensive threat. These batters, fortunately are in the minority in high school. In these particular cases the pitcher figures that even if he loses the batter and walks him he is not too bad off.

Situations

To further clarify the use of our plan of pitching strategy, different situations are presented as examples. It is impossible, of course, to present every conceivable situation that might occur, but several important ones are chosen to serve as guide lines for you to follow in adjusting your individual plan of attack.

Winning run on second. In this situation with a better than average hitter at bat the pitcher should pitch him fine and extra fine only. With first base unoccupied if the batter walks not much damage is done.

Winning run on first. With the winning run on first the pitcher does not want to walk the batter, putting the winning run on second, so he should lean toward percentage pitching and try to get the batter to hit the ball on the ground.

Four run lead, sixth inning. Analyze the offensive strategy, chances are they will be taking a strike. In this case the pitcher should pitch percentage most of the way. Make them hit you to beat you.

Bunt situation. Pitch fine, high, on first pitch and then pitch percentage preferably fast balls, high and hard to force the bunter to pop the ball up.

Hit and run situation. The hit and run is usually used by the offense when the pitcher is in the vulnerable position, three balls and one strike or two balls, and no strikes. If the pitcher has good control he can try to keep the ball inside on the batter. As mentioned before when the pitcher is vulnerable he must get the ball over.

Double play situation. Pitch fine until behind in the count attempting to get the batter to hit the ball on the ground by keeping the ball low.

Important runner on third less than two outs. Pitch fine all the way trying to keep the ball low and inside, especially if you do not have a good strike out pitch. The pitcher is guarding against the run scoring fly ball and the ground ball to the opposite side.

Additional principles of strategy

There are several miscellaneous principles that are very important for the pitcher and the coach to bear in mind when planning their strategy.

The set pattern. The pitcher should not fall into the habit of following a set pattern of pitching. Examples of this are: always throwing fast balls until ahead, throwing his best pitch until getting a strike, and only throwing breaking pitches and off-speed pitches when there is no pressure. There are many different types of patterns that the pitcher might fall into that can be avoided by carefully analyzing the pitching charts after the game.

Vary the pitches. Do not throw the same pitch in the same area too often.

Do not show everything. The pitcher should save his extra pitches for opportune spots. We have given examples throughout the book that illustrate this point.

Strength vs. strength. The bases are loaded, tie ball game, and the count is three balls and two strikes. The pitcher's best pitch is his fast ball and the hitter is a good fast ball hitter. Should the pitcher try to get the batter with his secondary pitch (weakness against weakness) or use his fast ball (strength against strength)? We recommend the pitcher pit his strength against the batter's strength. If the pitcher's strength is not good enough it is still better to get beat using his best rather than "throwing up" his secondary pitch. Of course, in our philosophy of pitching, we would hope that the pitcher's so-called secondary pitch actually would be as strong as his best pitch. In this case he would still be able to pitch to the batter's weakness with his strength.

The asking principle. We close our chapter on strategy with this important principle. We want our pitchers to ask themselves, Why?, What?, How?, and Where? before delivering each pitch. If they do not have the answer they should not throw the pitch. There *must* be a *reason* for throwing each pitch. The object of this entire chapter is to help the pitcher to be able to answer the all-important question, "Why am I throwing this pitch?"

◆ The Pitcher as a Fielder

ten

The pitcher must be considered the fifth infielder on the team. Some pitchers seem to think that their job is finished when they throw the pitch. The pitcher who is conscious of his fielding responsibilities can save many a ball game for himself and the team.

Some pitchers possess a great amount of poise and always seem ready to make the right play. Other pitchers appear nervous and shaky, unable ever to do the right thing. Spectators often call the latter type pitcher a choke artist. As mentioned before, we feel it is the coach's responsibility to make certain that his pitchers know how to deal with every conceivable defensive situation. He must make certain that they execute, over and over, all the plays to be made under all possible conditions. If the pitcher knows what to do and has done it many times in practice he very likely will be able to do it in the game.

PROPER POSITION TO FIELD

To be a good defensive man the pitcher must finish his follow-through in a squared position ready to charge ahead or to either side (Illustration 16, page 166). The pitcher should have in mind that the ball is going to be hit right back at him and that he must be alert and ready to field any type ball. The back or pivot foot should end up opposite the striding foot the weight balanced equally on each foot ready to field. *Balance* is the key to good fielding. You can help the pitcher who has difficulty assuming this fielding position by having him take an additional small step with his stride foot to get his feet parallel. He should not be so conscious of this that he loses his stuff.

165

Illustration 16
Pitcher's Fielding Position

COVERING FIRST BASE

Covering first base is one of the most important maneuvers for the pitcher to learn. On any ball hit to the left of the pitcher he should automatically break off the mound toward first base. To cover first base the pitcher should run directly to a point on the base line approximately ten feet from the bag. He should then round off giving the first baseman a good target to throw to. The shortest distance between two points is a straight line, and the pitcher can get the job done much quicker by running directly to the line and then rounding off for the throw. The pitcher should be cautioned not to run across the bag or run directly down the line because the runner will run over him.

The throw should be taken chest high about two steps before getting to the bag. If for some reason the pitcher gets to the bag ahead of the throw he must stop at the bag and become a first baseman, waiting for the throw. This often is the case when a throw is fumbled by an infielder. After receiving the throw and tagging the base the pitcher should turn into the diamond and face the infield ready to make a possible play on another runner. The pitcher should attempt to tag the bag with his right foot.

COVERING HOME

Covering home is more a matter of alertness than skill. Any time the catcher is drawn away from home plate the pitcher must be ready to cover. When there is a man on third base and a wild pitch or passed ball occurs, the pitcher must be alert to cover the plate. The same is true when the catcher leaves his position to go after a pop foul with a man in scoring position. If the pitcher does not cover the plate in this situation the runner can tag up after the catch and score.

The pitcher, if at all possible, should stay to the first base side of the plate when covering. He should be careful not to expose his back or pitching arm to the runner.

COVERING THE OTHER BASES

The pitcher should be made aware of the fact that he is not out on the mound to serve as a spectator. If an infielder leaves a base uncovered, for any reason, the pitcher must be ready to cover the base. Bases are usually left uncovered when two infielders are both chasing a pop fly.

FIELDING BUNTS AND SLOW ROLLERS

The main cause of unsuccessfully fielding bunts and slow rollers is taking one's eyes off the ball. The ball rolls slowly along the ground and about a foot from the glove the pitcher takes his eyes off the ball and bobbles it. The pitcher must be instructed to watch the ball into the glove, and then worry about making the throw.

On balls tapped to the first base side of the right handed pitcher the ball should be fielded with the glove ahead of the ball using the bare hand to scoop the ball into the glove. He should then straighten up, do a two-step and throw the ball accurately to the base. On balls to the third base side of the right handed pitcher, the ball should be fielded in front of the right foot and the pitcher should push off his right foot as he throws. The pitcher should not attempt to make this throw when off balance. On balls hit to the first base side of the left handed pitcher the pitcher should overrun the ball, spin on his left foot and make the throw. On balls hit to the third base side he must make a full pivot clockwise before throwing to first.

The first baseman can be a great aid to the pitcher when he is throwing to first. The first baseman should yell inside or outside and should give the pitcher a good target to throw to. The pitcher should take a short jag step or two step, before throwing the ball. This gives him a chance to spot the target and get his balance before throwing.

GETTING THE MAN AT SECOND BASE

The pitcher must know who is going to cover second on a ball hit back to him. With a runner on first he should always ask the second baseman and shortstop who is going to cover on a ball hit back to him. This should be a definite *rule!*

Getting the man at second is the all important consideration in this play. If the player covering the base sees that it is going to be close and he only has a chance for the force, he should place his foot on the diamond side of the bag, and stretch toward the throw the same as a first baseman does. This also gives the pitcher a good target toward which to throw.

On slow hit balls the catcher directs the play. The pitcher must keep his eye on the ball to field it and does not have time to look around and decide where to throw it. The catcher directs the pitcher by yelling second, or first. No other words are added because in the noise of the game it is often very difficult to distinguish the catcher's commands.

On hard hit balls back to the pitcher, with a man on first, the pitcher automatically throws to second base unless he fumbles the ball or the catcher yells otherwise. On double play balls, the ball should be thrown to the man covering the bag, chest high, leading the shortstop slightly or throwing the ball to the second baseman so that he can make his pivot. The important point is for the pitcher not to hurry his throw or make his throw off balance, but to concentrate on making his throw accurately.

GETTING THE MAN AT THIRD BASE

The slow hit ball or bunt down the third base line with runners on first and second is one of the hardest plays for the defense to handle. The big play for the defense in this situation, is to get the lead runner going into third. If this is impossible it is imperative that an out be recorded at first base or second base.

In this situation the pitcher is responsible for fielding the bunt or slow roller hit to his third base side. The third baseman covers the base for the throw from the pitcher that forces the runner going to third. If the catcher sees that the play cannot be made at third, because of a big jump by the runner or the pitcher fumbling the ball, he yells first or second immediately.

The third baseman is the key to the play. The minute the ball is hit or bunted he must make the decision as to whether the pitcher can field the ball. If there is any thought in his mind that the pitcher cannot field the ball he immediately yells, "I got it!" and makes the play at first or second base. Once the pitcher hears the third baseman yell, he must relinquish his fielding responsibility and let the third baseman field it, and make his play. If the pitcher tries to field it there is no one covering third anyway, and he will have difficulty making the play at first. If the third baseman sees that the pitcher *can* field the ball he hustles back to the bag, stretches into the infield like a first baseman, and gives the pitcher a good target to throw to, for the force out. The pitcher must be careful not to make an inaccurate throw, as a bad throw here will usually let in two runs. The play is to get the force out at third, and to do this, the pitcher must practice getting off the mound in a hurry and making an accurate throw to the third baseman.

DEFENSIVE DRILLS

To do a good job on defense the pitcher must be drilled repeatedly so that his actions become automatic. Daily drills and an understanding of their execution is the key to developing a good fielding pitcher. These drills are presented in chapter twelve.

We should like to mention the all-purpose defensive drill as an example of a drill that should be performed everyday of practice. This drill includes covering first, getting the force at second, getting the double play, and getting the force at third. This entire drill using five or six pitchers, the catcher, and the whole infield can be executed in ten minutes and pays large dividends. The pitcher practices fielding slow rollers, swinging bunts, line drives, hard hit ground balls and also practices how and where to throw the ball under various conditions and situations.

HANDLING POP FLIES

There should be a definite team rule for handling pop flies that covers all possible situations. Our rule is that the "in man" has the ball until the "deep man" calls him off. As an example, if the pop fly is hit over shortstop, the shortstop has the ball until the outfielder calls him off. The shortstop may run all the way to the fence if he is not called off. The same rule applies between the catcher and third baseman, second baseman and right fielder, etc.

The discussion always arises as to whether the pitcher should be allowed to catch pop flies. We would rather have an infielder catch the pop fly in most cases as he usually has the ball in front of him and is more adept at catching pop flies. The pitcher is responsible for catching pop flies in the vicinity of the mound until he is called off if he can make the catch easily. How many times have you seen the pitcher turn his back and walk off the mound as the third baseman rushes in madly only to see the ball plop right in the middle of the mound? This is ridiculous! Most pitchers are good enough athletes to walk one or two feet and catch a pop fly.

BACKING UP THE BASES

After the ball is hit, the pitcher gets in the way if he remains on the mound. He has a definite defensive job to fulfill, and it is *not* standing on the mound as an observer. The pitcher is *not* to act as a cut-off man on any play. Many times we have seen a pitcher who is supposed to be behind the catcher, stand between the catcher and the mound and get in the way, or cut off a throw, that might otherwise have gotten the runner.

The object in having a pitcher back up the base is to have someone in back of the infielder or catcher to stop the ball in case of a bad throw or bad bounce. The pitcher who backs up the play from a distance of five or ten feet is of little value, as the ball will probably bounce by him also. The pitcher should be at least twenty-five feet behind any base he is backing up, and should be ready to block the ball to keep it from getting by, allowing the runner to take an extra base.

Anticipating

The pitcher must be able to anticipate where a possible play may be made. He must think one base ahead of the runner. He must be able to observe, anticipate, and move in a split second. To aid the pitcher in determining where to go in different situations we have broken the rule into three headings, (1) backing up third, (2) backing up home, and (3) positioning between third and home.

Backing up third. The pitcher should back up third in the following situations: (1) with a runner on first base and a hit to the outfield, (2) with a runner on second base and a fly ball to the outfield, (3) with runners on first and third and a hit to the outfield, (4) with runners on first and second and a fly ball to the outfield, and (5) an infield error with runners on first base or first and second base.

Backing up home. The pitcher should back up home in the following situations: (1) with a runner on second base and a hit to the outfield, (2) with runners on second and third and a hit to the outfield, and (3) with runners on first and third base and a fly ball to the outfield.

Positioning between third and home. The position between third and home is called the decision spot. The pitcher stations himself between third and home until he can determine if a play is going to be made on the lead runner. The pitcher should position himself between third and home in the following situations: (1) with runners on first and second base and a hit to the outfield, (2) with runners on second and third base and a fly ball to the outfield, (3) with bases loaded and a hit to the outfield, and (4) with a runner on first and an extra base hit.

HOLDING THE RUNNER ON FIRST

Holding the runner close to first is very important to the team defense. Second base is usually stolen on the pitcher not the catcher. The pitcher must develop a good move to keep the runner from getting a jump.

The runner

The runners should be studied carefully to detect any give away sign, that they might be going to steal. The pitcher should know the runner's characteristics as well as he knows the hitters. The runner may tip his hand by leaning toward the next base, varying his lead when he is going to steal, pointing his front foot toward the next base or by any number of tell-tale signs that may be characteristic of the particular runner. The pitcher should not allow the runner to get a walking start, but make him stop before he delivers the ball to the plate.

Knowing the opponent

The pitcher must be aware of the other team's offensive philosophy and pattern of play. The pitcher should know from the scouting reports which players are more apt to run and in which situations they usually run. If the pitcher has a thorough knowledge of the opponent's capabilities and pattern of strategy, it will help him to deal more effectively with the base runner.

Pitching from the stretch

The pitcher must develop a motion from the stretch, that does not tip when he is going to the plate and when he is going to first. He must constantly work to make everything look the same. Baserunners are always studying the pitcher's actions to find out if he does anything that might tip his move. The pitcher must avoid such mannerisms as lifting his front leg higher when going to the plate, leaning toward the runner when he is going to throw to first, or any other nervous mannerism that might tip his move.

The pitcher *must* vary his looks to keep the runner honest. Some pitchers are easy to steal on, because they only look once, or they always look at the runner the same number of times, before throwing to the plate.

The pitcher must avoid exaggerating his leg kick with a man on first. The motion should be rapid and the front foot kept close to the ground, or the runner will be able to get a big jump. As the pitcher must work hard to make every pitch look the same, he also must work diligently to make his motion when going to the plate, look the same as when he is throwing to first.

PICKING THE RUNNER OFF FIRST

One of the greatest secrets in picking a runner off first base or any base, is knowing *when* to throw. If the pitcher catches the runner either leaning, jumping, or with his feet crossed, he does not have to have a great move to pick the runner off. The pitcher should watch the runner for these mistakes.

The pitcher should vary his manner and speed of throwing to first base. He may throw over to first using a bad move, and then pick the runner off with his good move. He may vary his technique by throwing over as soon as he gets the ball back from the catcher, as soon as he steps on the rubber, or throwing again to first, immediately after receiving the ball from the first baseman. The left handed pitcher, of course, has the advantage, as he is facing the runner and can make his move much more deceptive than the right hander.

PICK-OFF PLAYS

Pick-off plays are used to keep the runners from getting big leads as well as to pick them off. A pick-off play is successful if it keeps the opposing runners close to the bases.

Pick-off at first—runners on first and second

This play is usually effective after an attempt has been made to pick-off the runner at second base. The runner on first is often watching what is going on at second and forgets that the first baseman may come behind him and pick him off.

When there are men on first and second, the pitcher is responsible for checking the shortstop, second baseman, and first baseman for a possible pick-off sign. On this particular play the pitcher has received no sign from the shortstop or second baseman so he looks at the first baseman and receives the sign, for the pick-off at first. As the first baseman hits his glove the pitcher looks back at second, and slowly counts to three, and then turns and throws to the first baseman coming in behind the runner. This play has proved to be very effective.

Pick-off at second base

The count play is also effective at second base. The second baseman gives the sign, runs toward second and when he plants his foot the pitcher and shortstop begin their count of three, as the second baseman runs back to his normal fielding position. On the count of three the pitcher pivots and throws to the shortstop coming in behind the runner. The pitcher is cautioned to count one while still looking at second, and two and three while facing the plate. If he does all his counting while facing the plate the play oftentimes is tipped because of the long wait. There are several variations of this play; the shortstop can initiate it with the second baseman covering, or the pitcher can throw directly to the first player that approaches the bag. The play with the shortstop coming behind the runner is effective because the runner sees the second baseman leave and has a tendency to relax as the shortstop sneaks in behind him. On pick-offs at second base the pitcher *should* not throw the ball if he sees the runner is back in, safely. The pitcher must also allow enough time, after the infielder has made a fake break, for him to get back to his defensive position before he pitches to the plate.

DEFENDING AGAINST THE SQUEEZE PLAY

The squeeze play is often used with a fast runner on third when one run is needed. In the suicide squeeze the runner breaks from third with the pitch and the batter must attempt to bunt the pitch no matter where it is. In the safe squeeze the runner does not break until he sees the ball is bunted on the ground, and the batter only attempts to bunt a strike. When using the suicide squeeze, if the ball is bunted at all, the runner will usually score, as he is breaking with the pitch.

The two best ways of defending against the squeeze, are (1) keeping the runner close to third base and (2) preventing the batter from bunting the ball.

Keeping the runner close to third

If the squeeze play is suspected the pitcher should pitch from his stretch position. There is a special defensive play that can be used in this situation. This play is more effective when a right hander is pitching. As the runner takes his lead off third, the third baseman walks up alongside him and stands there until the pitcher brings his hands down in the stretch and looks at him. When the pitcher looks at the runner the third baseman breaks back toward third base. If the runner does not break back toward third with the third baseman, the pitcher whirls and throws to third to pick the runner off. If the runner does break back for third, the pitcher throws to the plate. The theory of this play is that the runner will have a difficult time scoring if he is going toward third as the ball is pitched.

Preventing the batter from bunting the ball

Some coaches want their pitcher to throw high and inside when the squeeze play is on. We prefer to have the pitcher throw low and inside to a right handed batter and low and outside to the left handed batter. Throwing low and inside still serves the purpose of driving the batter back and makes the tag easier for the catcher. If the squeeze play is on, any previous signal is disregarded and the pitcher throws a fast ball. The pitcher must be cautious not to change his normal delivery once he has started his motion or a balk will be called.

DEFENDING AGAINST THE STEAL OF HOME

Home is stolen on the pitcher. The runner must have a good lead or a walking start to steal home. If there is a fast runner on third base and the steal of home is suspected the pitcher should pitch from his stretch. Again, it is important to know the capabilities of the opposition.

If the pitcher gets the sign and then looks at the runner before pitching, it is very difficult for the runner to get the good jump and steal home. We make it a definite rule that the pitcher do this, with a runner on third. If the steal is on, the pitch should be a fast ball, low and inside to the right handed batter and low and outside to the left handed batter, as in the defense against the squeeze play.

DEFENDING AGAINST THE DELAYED STEAL

The delayed steal is worked with runners on first and third. When the pitcher takes his stretch and looks at first the runner on first breaks for second. He is trying to draw the throw, to allow the runner to score from third, or force the pitcher to balk, by getting him to move his shoulder toward first and then not completing the throw. The runner on third is instructed to run, the minute the pitcher turns his shoulder or throws toward first.

We have devised a defense for this particular offensive play that works effectively. As soon as the runner breaks for second the pitcher steps *back* off the rubber turns toward second and takes a step as if to go after the runner, decoying the runner on third to break for the plate. After taking this one step, the pitcher whirls and gets the runner going home. This play must be made quickly so as not to allow the runner to get too big a jump toward the plate.

DEFENDING AGAINST THE DOUBLE STEAL

The double steal is performed with runners on first and third. This is one of the most difficult plays against which to defend. The runner on first breaks with the pitch and with less than two outs attempts to steal second, with two outs he stops before getting to the bag and tries to remain in the run-down long enough to allow the runner on third to score. The runner on third is usually instructed to break for the plate when the throw from the catcher goes past the pitcher.

We have four basic plays for preventing the double steal. The pitcher must be aware of these plays. On all of them the catcher must glance at the runner on third before throwing through. If he does not do this, none of the plays will work, as the runner will get too big a jump. On all the plays the catcher must throw the ball through the pitcher, head high, with something on it.

Fake and throw to third

On this play the catcher must make a full motion fake of throwing through to second base. He fakes the throw bringing the ball down by the side of his right leg and then throws to third.

Throw back to the pitcher

This is sometimes called a bush play but it has worked many times. The catcher throws the ball hard at the pitcher's head who catches it and fires to third. The success of the play depends upon how much it looks like the throw is going all the way through to second base.

All the way through

When the ball is thrown all the way through to second base we have one infielder, usually the second baseman, responsible for handling the throw. If he sees the runner break or the third baseman lets him know the runner is going home, he can cut the ball off and throw to the plate. If not, he remains at second and makes the tag on the runner coming into second base. We prefer this play to the one in which an infielder is the cut-off man and the other covers the bag because of the confusion often resulting between the second baseman and shortstop. We like to have one player responsible for the entire operation.

Cut-off man

This play has proved to be successful. It is used when the runner on third is very important. In this play the entire emphasis is upon getting the man at the plate. As the pitch is made the second baseman comes in to a position about fifteen feet behind the mound. The throw will go through the pitcher to the second baseman, who has a short throw to the catcher. Remember, the runner has been told to run when the ball goes by the pitcher, and this play fakes him into running home where he can be thrown out by the second baseman's relative short throw.

THE BALK

The balk rule allows the base runner to advance to the next base when the pitcher has committed a rule transgression. The balk rule is complicated, so let us look at some of the ways the balk might be prevented:

1. The pitcher must not drop the ball in the middle of his delivery.
2. When the pitcher wants to chase down a runner he must step *back* off the rubber, thus becoming an infielder.
3. The pitcher must make no pretense to pitch when he does not have the ball.
4. The pitcher must step directly toward where he is going to throw.
5. Once the pitcher has started his motion to the plate he must complete it.
6. Once the pitcher has started his motion to first base he must complete it.
7. The pitcher must have his foot in contact with the rubber when pitching.
8. The pitcher must pause for one second in the stretch position, before delivering the ball to the plate.

◆ Scouting and
the Use of Charts

eleven

As in any learning situation the pitcher never stops developing. It is a continuous process. Some coaches do an outstanding job of developing their pitchers but because small details are overlooked in the process, the pitchers never seem to reach their optimum level of performance. The truly outstanding coach is the one who attends to every minute detail, no matter how unimportant it may seem. In this chapter we shall present some of the important aids to pitching success that are so often overlooked.

SCOUTING

Scouting is very important in any type competition. The salesman in a sense scouts his opponent when he goes over the prospective customer's needs, probable objections, and reception to methods of motivation. The successful salesman does not go into a transaction without careful preliminary preparation and a plan of attack. The salesman, general, or coach who does not do this preliminary work is cutting his chances of success to a minimum. We feel it is foolish to put years of work into developing a pitcher and then have him fail because we are too busy to scout and size up our opponent.

Methods of scouting

Two competent scouts should be sent out to scout an opponent. In many cases there is no money in the budget for baseball scouting. We have had considerable success using former players, or players that are injured, or otherwise ineligible. The scouting is more efficient if the people doing the scouting are acquainted with your particular ball club and philosophy of play. If they are aware of your pitcher's strengths and weaknesses they are better able to evaluate the opponent within a frame of reference that is more useful to you. As mentioned in chapter nine, the batting practice period can also be helpful in analyzing the hitter.

Scouting charts should be used! When not used, much time is wasted, and often the scouts come away from the game with little information. In our own work, we ask our scouts to summarize the information after the game and then bring it to us. We go over the information with them while the game is still fresh in their minds. If a day or two elapses between the game and the discussion of the information, many of the details may be forgotten.

Scouting charts

Scouting charts should be designed so that they are easy to use, not cumbersome, and yet designed to provide all the necessary information. If they are too complicated to use and to interpret they are of little value. In constructing charts the coach must decide what he wants to learn from them, how the observations can be most simply recorded, and how the results can be interpreted. Much thought has gone into the construction of our charts and we have found them to be very valuable to our program. The charts are not complicated and can easily be handled by two scouts, even by one, in a pinch. The two charts will be discussed separately, but after the game they are evaluated together. By using the two charts you can become thoroughly acquainted with the hitters' strengths and weaknesses.

On this chart every pitch thrown the batter is recorded by the scout. The summary of all pitches made is recorded under

NAME: *JOE SMITH* BATS: *R* OPP. PITCHER: *STEVE BROWN* L. OR R.: *R*
SYMBOLS: F--fast ball Ch--change G.B.--ground ball F.B.--fly ball
C--curve ball Kn--knuckle ball L.D.--line drive Fo--foul
H--hit P.F.--pop fly.

Inning-①23456789 BR-123	Inning-12③456789 BR-123	Inning-123④56789 BR-1②③
/ F.Fo.L.D. PULL ▣	/ C ▣	/ F-Sw ▣
/ C ▣	/ Ch ▣	/ -C ▢
/ C ▣	/ C ▣	/ C ▣
F. P.F. ▣	/ Side A-F-Fo ▣	/ C-Sw-Ⓚ ▢
▢	/ C ▢	▢
▢	/ F-L.D. SINGLE ▢	▢

Inning-123456⑦89 BR-123	Inning-123456789 BR-123
/ F. double ▣	/ C ▣
▢	/ C ▣
▢	/ Side ARM C. Foul-PULL ▢
▢	/ F ▢
▢	/ C P.F.-SS ▢

	no.of ptch's	no.of strk's	no.of taken strk's	no. of hits	k'd on	ground out-on	flied out on	lined out on	popped up	fouled off	bad p. swing at	ptch's pulled
Fast b.	6	3	0	2	0	0	0	0	/	/	2	4
Curve	11	/	6	0	/	0	0	0	/	0	/	/
Change	/	0	0	0	0	0	0	0	0	0	0	0
Side A-F	/	/	0	0	0	0	0	0	0	/	/	0
Side A-C	/	/	0	0	0	0	0	0	0	/	0	/
Knuckle	0	0	0	0	0	0	0	0	0	0	0	0
Totals	20	6	6	2	/	0	0	0	2	3	4	6

ANSWER FOLLOWING ON THE BACK: (Guide questions only--record any
other pertinent information.)

1. Was there any trend on pitches missed, hit, popped up, pulled etc.?
2. Did he hit better or worse with certain count or counts?
3. Greatest strength and weakness.
4. What did hitter do with men on base?
5. What pitch did he swing at the most, take the most, etc.?
6. Conclusions: (Drawn from chart and information.)

their respective categories and the conclusions are drawn from this. To facilitate your understanding of the use of this chart you may refer to it as we take you through a hypothetical case. The markings which are a result of the actions of this particular batter are already recorded for you in the illustration.

First time at bat. The first pitch was an inside fast ball that was a line-drive foul, down the third base line for strike one. (Note where pitch is marked in the square.) The second pitch was a curve ball low and outside for ball one. The third pitch was a curve down the middle for a called strike. The fourth pitch was an outside fast ball which the batter tried to pull and popped up to third. (Note, marking number one in right hand square.)

Second time at bat. The first pitch was a curve down the middle taken for a strike. The second pitch was a low change-up taken for a ball. The third pitch was a curve taken down the middle for a strike. The next pitch was a side-arm fast ball, outside, that was fouled off. The fifth pitch was a low curve taken for ball two. The next pitch was an inside fast ball hit for a clean single down the left field line.

Third time at bat. It was the fourth inning and there were runners on second and third. (Note upper box.) The first pitch was a high fast ball missed for a strike. The second pitch was a low curve ball taken for a ball. The next pitch was a curve down the middle taken for a strike. The fourth pitch was a curve low, swung at, and missed.

Fourth time at bat. The first pitch was a fast ball hit up against the fence for a double.

Fifth time at bat. The first pitch was a curve taken for a strike. The second pitch was a curve down the middle taken for a strike. The third pitch was a side arm curve pulled foul. The fourth pitch was a low fast ball taken for a ball. The fifth pitch was an outside curve ball popped up to the shortstop.

Summary. After the game each batter's performance is summarized on the chart. We have done this for you.

Conclusions from the chart. The batter did not swing at the curve until he had two strikes on him. He tried to pull everything, even outside pitches. He swung at the first pitch whenever it was a fast ball. He pulled the fast ball to left field solidly. He popped up outside pitches twice, trying to pull the ball. The only fast ball he missed was the high fast ball. His strength seemed to be pulling the fast ball, and his weakness seemed to be trying to pull the outside pitch, and taking the curve up to two strikes. From this chart it is recommended that the batter be given the curve for a strike on the first pitch, followed by another breaking pitch. The pitcher should keep everything outside. The pitcher with the good fast ball may be able to throw it past him, high.

If you will refer to chart number two you will find that what is recorded is self-explanatory, derived from what the scout has observed.

Pitching plan

We now combine the two charts and formulate our pitching plan for each batter, after analyzing our pitcher's wares and analyzing the batter. As you can see by glancing at the charts we have a pretty good idea on how to pitch this particular hitter.

Cautions

If there does not seem to be a decisive trend shown on the charts do not try to invent one. As is sometimes the case, one game may not give you enough information to formulate a complete pitching plan. There usually is enough information derived, however, to help you pitch to the batter with some idea of his strengths and weaknesses.

The major caution is not to become so involved with the

SCOUTING CHART NUMBER TWO

Name *Joe Smith* BATS *R* OPP. PITCHER *Steve Brown* L. or R. *R*

Two sentence description of pitcher: *The pitcher has a good curve and is "sneaky" fast.*

Batter's mental characteristics. (Nervous, lazy, confident, guesser, etc.) Classify and comment. *Looks confident and is patient to wait for his pitch. Anticipates fast-ball until he has two strikes. Reluctant to swing at anything but fast-ball.*

GRIP: choke (how far?)_____ END: *X*_____ STRIDE: In:_____ Away: *X*

LENGTH: *long stride* STANCE: open:_____ closed: *slightly* Straight-up: *X*

crouch:_____ narrow: *X* wide:_____ distance from plate: *close*

BAT: thin handle *X* thick handle_____ .HANDS: high *X* low:_____

WRISTS: quick *X* lazy:_____ . BAT POSITION: high *X* flat:_____

SWING: hitch _____ free swing: *X* pushes ball_____ uppercuts: *slight*

describe swing: *Swings bat from end, golfs low pitch, good wrist action*

MAJOR FLAWS: *Tries to pull everything, including outside pitch. May have trouble with high fast pitch.*

STRENGTHS: *Good fast-ball hitter. Pulls fast ball well, waits for his pitch.*

SUBJECTIVE DESCRIPTION OF HITTER: *Aggressive pull hitter, first pitch swinging on fast ball. Good power, free swinger.*

RECOMMENDED PITCHING PLAN (Bear in mind our pitcher): *Throw him breaking stuff to get ahead. Keep fast-ball outside. Pitch him away and may throw him high. Put something on first pitch. Change up on him as he can be caught off balance.*

opposition's weaknesses that you forget your own pitcher's strengths. Do not weaken your pitcher's technique and mode of pitching by overscouting and overconcentrating on the opposition. The major object of the thorough scouting report is to be able to pitch to your opponent with a degree of intelligence. *Paying attention to small details wins ball games.* The mimeographing of the forms, and the little time that goes into their interpretation, is well worth the effort.

THE USE OF PITCHING CHARTS

We mentioned previously that the coach should not spend so much time scouting and analyzing the opposition that he forgets about analyzing his own pitcher's performance. It is also a part of the pitcher's duty to carefully scrutinize his own performance. He cannot do this from memory. His efforts must be recorded in an organized manner so that he can efficiently evaluate his turn on the mound.

Purposes of the pitching charts

There are four general purposes of the pitching charts.

To analyze the pitcher's performance. When the pitcher completes his turn on the mound his job is not finished. If any learning is to take place he must carefully analyze and evaluate his total performance. This cannot be done by just trying to recall from memory what he has done. We have him pick up the pitcher's recording chart along with the pitcher's summary sheet (to be discussed below) and carefully go over his performance. The pitcher's recording sheet has already been filled out by a pitcher who did not pitch. After a brief discussion with the coach, he takes the two charts home, completes them, draws his conclusions, and the next morning turns them into the coach for further scrutinization. After the coach has had time to go over the charts the pitcher is called in and the final evaluation and suggestions are made. There is no guess work in the process, as the pitcher knows where he was weak and where he was strong, and knows what he must spend time on in order to improve.

To get the pitcher thinking. One of the most difficult problems for the coach is to get the young pitcher to *concentrate* and to do a more professional job. The charts motivate him to be precise in his pitching and to have a reason for every move he makes.

To develop confidence. The charts help give the pitcher confidence in what he is doing, and help him feel more professional in going about his duties. He knows he is on a team that is going about its job of beating the other team in a successful manner. He knows his own strengths and weaknesses as well as the opposition's. He can check between innings and find out exactly what he threw in each situation. No stone has been left unturned in helping him deal successfully with each hitter.

To motivate improvement. Many times, winning signifies improvement to the pitcher, and losing signifies failure. There is more to evaluating the pitcher's improvement than going over his won and lost record. By using the charts, the pitcher can observe his improvement, or lack of improvement objectively. Because all his pitches are recorded and summarized, he strives to improve on his weaknesses even though he may be winning most of his games. Pitchers who are winning oftentimes are not motivated to improve unless a device such as the charts is employed. Conversely, a pitcher who is losing can use the charts to evaluate his performance and can oftentimes gain satisfaction from the fact that he is showing constant improvement.

The pitcher's recording sheet

The pitcher's recording sheet is completed in the same manner as scouting chart number one. Each large squared section represents one time at bat for each hitter. The records of the hitters are kept consecutively throughout the game. It usually takes about five or six recording sheets to record one game. As an example of how to record, refer to the illustration on which we have recorded the actions of the first hitter.

First batter. The first pitch to Smith, a right handed batter, was a fast ball low and outside for a ball. The second pitch was

a curve down the middle swung at and missed. The third pitch
was a change off the fast ball and taken for a strike, at the knees.
The next pitch was a fast ball at the knees, swung at and missed
for strike three.

PITCHER'S RECORDING SHEET

B	S	Batter L-Ⓡ *Smith* / Baserunner 1-2-3 / Inning ①23456789	B	S	Batter L-Ⓡ *Doe* / Baserunner 1-2-3 / Inning ①23456789	B	S	Batter Ⓛ-R *Jones* / Baserunner 1-2-3 / Inning ①23456789
/		F.B. ☐.			☐			☐
	/	C – sw ☐•			☐			☐
	/	Ch off F.B. ☐•			☐			☐
	/	F.B,–sw Ⓡ ☐•			☐			☐
		☐			☐			☐
		☐			☐			☐

B	S	Batter Ⓛ-R *Jackson* / Baserunner 1-2-3 / Inning 1②3456789	B	S	Batter Ⓛ-R *Ross* / Baserunner 1-2-3 / Inning 1②3456789	B	S	Batter L-Ⓡ *Gregory* / Baserunner 1-2-3 / Inning 1②3456789
		☐			☐			☐
		☐			☐			☐
		☐			☐			☐
		☐			☐			☐
		☐			☐			☐
		☐			☐			☐

B	S	Batter L-Ⓡ *Clark* / Baserunner 1-2-3 / Inning 12③456789	B	S	Batter Ⓛ-R *Carr* / Baserunner ①-2-3 / Inning 12③456789	B	S	Batter L-Ⓡ *Langton* / Baserunner ①-②-3 / Inning 12③456789
		☐			☐			☐
		☐			☐			☐
		☐			☐			☐
		☐			☐			☐
		☐			☐			☐
		☐			☐			☐

The next eight batters. We have not attempted to record each
pitch to each batter in the illustration, as the recording is done
in the same manner as in scouting chart number one. We call
your attention, however, to the methods used for marking the

number of men on base, the inning, and whether the batter is a left or right handed batter.

The pitcher's summary sheet

When the pitcher has completed his turn on the mound he picks up the recording sheets and a pitcher's summary sheet on which to record and summarize his performance. This process should involve approximately an hour's work at home. We have summarized a hypothetical performance for you in the illustration. Note how each pitch is transcribed from the pitcher's recording sheet to the pitching plot so that the pitcher in a glance can see where he was throwing his pitches. Each type pitch is summarized on the chart using information gathered from the pitcher's recording sheet.

The questions at the bottom of the summary sheet act as guide points for the pitcher's evaluation. He should attempt to answer these questions and others that might be relevant, on the back of the chart. From the summary sheet try to answer as many questions as you can about the pitcher's performance. To find out if he was pitching by any set pattern the recording sheet is consulted. Below are listed just a few of the conclusions that might be drawn from the chart.

1. The best pitch was his fast ball. His control of it was the best, and he kept it low.
2. He mixed his fast ball and curve pretty well on the first pitch, but did not rely on any other pitch in this situation.
3. He relied upon his fast ball in all tight situations.
4. For the most part, he kept all of his pitches low.
5. He had control problems with his curve, usually low and outside.
6. He can improve by working on his secondary pitches so that he can use them on two balls and no strikes, three balls and one strike, and three balls and two strikes.
7. His worst mistake was the high change-up fast ball hit for a homerun.

Name___J. Jones___ TEAMS _Union_ vs. _Central_ No. of batters __35__

	no. of ptch's	no. of strk's	no. of balls	pitch hit for outs	pitch hit for b. hit	pitch used for K	pitch used for first pitch	pitch used for 2 balls & 0 strikes
FAST BALL	70	49	21	13	2	6	21	4
CURVE BALL	30	12	18	3	3	1	14	0
CHANGE-UP F.B.	12	8	4	2	1-HR.	1	0	0
CHANGE-UP Curve	10	7	3	1	0	0	0	0
SIDEARM-F.B.	0	0	0	0	0	0	0	0
SIDEARM-CURVE	0	0	0	0	0	0	0	0
OTHER PITCHES	0	0	0	0	0	0	0	0
TOTALS	122	76	46	19	6	8	35	4

	ptch's used 3 & 1	ptch's used 3 & 2
FAST BALL	4	5
CURVE BALL	1	0
CHANGE-UP F.B.	1	0
CHANGE-UP Curve	0	0
SIDEARM-F.B.	0	0
SIDEARM-CURVE	0	0
OTHER PITCHES	0	0
TOTALS	6	5

PITCHING PLOT

POINTS TO LOOK FOR IN EVALUATION:

1. What was best pitch? Why?

2. Was same pitch used on first pitch too often?

3. Was each type pitch thrown where you wanted it?

4. If had control problems--which pitch and where?

5. Were you pitching by any set pattern?

6. Which pitch was hit the hardest?

7. Which pitch was used in clutch situations the most?

8. Ideas for improvement.

For ease of reading, different colored pencils can be used to mark each type pitch on the pitching plot with a dot.

The test

Tests should be designed to meet your individual coaching situation. The test is given to find out where each pitcher needs more work on theory, where you may have been weak in your coaching, and to make certain the pitcher has the basic information needed to do a successful job of pitching. A pitcher cannot pitch in a game until he has passed the test 100%. He may take it as many times as necessary.

The test should include items that you want to make sure the pitcher knows before he takes the mound. The test should reflect the step by step process you have used in developing your pitcher.

The project

The project is presented in notebook form and the answers to the test questions are included in it. It should be set up to meet specific needs of the coach. A sample project is presented below for your information.

1. Write a one page philosophy of pitching.
2. Outline a conditioning program for off-season, pre-season, and during season periods.
3. What type pitcher are you? How did you reach these conclusions?
4. Describe three different type hitters and explain how you would pitch to each one. (You may use three of our hitters if you wish.)
5. Diagram and explain our basic pick-off plays.
6. Explain the four basic categories under which the various counts fall.
7. Considering your self-evaluation, place each count under one of the four categories and describe which pitches you would use in each category.
8. Describe the push-button principle.

9. Describe your favorite professional pitcher, paying particular attention to his strengths, weaknesses, techniques, pattern of pitching, *etc.*
10. Explain the strength vs. strength and weakness vs. weakness principle.
11. Include in your notebook any illustrative pictures you see in magazines or newspapers that represent good form.
12. References.

♦ Pitching Drills

twelve

Repetition accompanied by understanding is the secret of learning any skill. Mere repetition, without understanding and explanation, is next to worthless. The same repetition of activity, day after day without variation, is monotonous and much of the benefit of the practice is lost.

To be a successful pitching coach you must have at your finger tips a number of drills that will enable you to vary your coaching approach from day to day. By inserting different drills to accomplish your purposes, practice can be maintained at an enthusiastic level.

In addition to helping you break up the monotonous routine of repetition, drills serve still another purpose. They allow you to approach the various skills from many different angles. By varying your drills you are providing the pitchers with a wider experience of activities from which to learn.

The drill must be carefully evaluated before it is incorporated into your scheme of teaching. Repeating a poor drill that is not meeting the purposes you have in mind is not only a waste of time, but can have negative results on the pitcher's performance. Before accepting a drill for use, you should figure out just what you want to get across, and then decide if this particular drill serves the purpose efficiently.

To aid in your coaching we have included thirty-three drills that serve definite purposes in the development of the successful pitcher. These drills have been tried and proven in developing the successful pitcher. The selection is wide enough to provide any particular drill that meets your pitcher's specific needs. They have been organized under four general headings: (1) Form and Delivery, (2) Mental Considerations, (3) Fielding, and (4) Conditioning. The purpose of each drill is explained and its place in the pitcher's development is described.

DRILLS FOR FORM AND DELIVERY

Developing proper form is largely a matter of establishing habits that the pitcher uses automatically in his delivery. Proper form can be more easily attained by making use of the (1) developmental drills and (2) those which we have presented for correcting poor pitching habits.

1. Drinking Glass Drill. (Illustration number nine page 95)

The drinking glass drill can be used at home to perfect proper hand and wrist action. The emphasis in this drill is upon loose wrist action from the lay back position, which is so important in developing a live ball. This drill should be used to correct the pitcher who pushes the ball when he throws.

Procedure. The pitcher extends his arm in the lay back position with the back of his hand facing up. He holds a glass (preferably plastic) lengthwise between his hand and his forearm, and with loose wrist action throws the glass into a couch or other soft object. The pitcher should practice this at least fifty times every night to develop the habit.

2. Back-of-Hand Up Drill. (Illustration number four page 80)

This drill is used in conjunction with the drinking glass drill to correct the pitcher who pushes the ball and has poor wrist action. If the back of the hand is facing up in the lay-back position it is very difficult to push the ball.

Procedure. This drill is used when actually throwing the ball to a catcher. The emphasis is upon having the back of the hand facing up when in the lay-back position. When this drill is first being initiated the pitcher should look back at his hand to see that it is in the proper position. After getting used to the action he can have a teammate or coach tell him whether the back of the hand is up. When the habit is firmly entrenched in the delivery the pitcher will be able to feel when he has done it correctly.

3. Driving Arm to Ground Drill. (Illustration number four page 80)

This drill is used to aid the development of a strong coiling action. By driving the arm down toward the ground in the lay-back position the catapulting action is aided. This drill aids the pitcher who does not get a good push off the rubber.

Procedure. The pitcher practices this action in front of a mirror or coach. The emphasis is upon driving the pitching arm down toward the ground in the lay-back position. After getting the feel of the action the pitcher should practice this drill daily while pitching to a catcher.

4. Hold Foot Back Drill.

This is an outstanding drill for correcting over-all form. Many times you will see a young pitcher who does not look right in his delivery. This drill combined with drill number five will help the young pitcher to look good sooner than any other method we know. This is an outstanding drill for developing strong hip action.

Procedure. The coach or another player lies outstretched on the ground behind the rubber and holds the pitcher's back foot on the rubber. The pitcher is told to pitch from his natural delivery and to throw the ball as hard as he can while his foot is held back. To throw the ball hard he will have to get his hips into the pitch and bend his back. After he has done this a number of times, he should practice it every day, holding his foot on the rubber through his own power. The pitcher should be cautioned not to over-stride.

5. Knee to Ground Drill. (Illustration number six page 84)

This drill should be used in conjunction with drill number four. It emphasizes getting the hips into the pitch. It is also an outstanding aid to get the pitcher to bend his back and to release the ball low and out in front. This drill may also be used to regulate a pitcher who is over-striding.

Procedure. The pitcher is instructed to *touch* his back knee on the ground as he pitches. He should do this many times until he gets the idea of driving his knee toward the ground and getting strong hip action. After he has done this he can pitch regularly with the emphasis still upon getting the back knee low. (Try drills four and five on any of your pitchers, you will be amazed at the quick results in the improvement in form.)

6. Center Line Drill. (Illustration number five page 82)

This drill is used to aid the pitcher in opening his hips and to keep him from throwing across his body.

Procedure. As the pitcher stands in his regular pitching position on the rubber, a line is drawn between his feet extending approximately five feet in front of the rubber. The right handed pitcher must plant his stride foot on, or to the left of the line, when he delivers the pitch. (Vice-versa for left handers.) If the pitcher's stride foot lands to the right of the line he is throwing across his body and is not getting the benefit of a powerful delivery. The pitcher must be cautioned not to open up too much (stride too far to the left of the line) as this will also dissipate much of his power. The spot on the ground where the pitcher's stride foot lands each time should be marked.

7. Hitting Coach's Hand Drill.

The purpose of this drill is to emphasize to the pitcher the importance of taking a natural stride rather than an exaggerated one.

Procedure. The coach positions himself three feet in front of the pitcher with the palm of his hand facing the pitcher. The pitcher is instructed to step and hit the coach's palm with his pitching hand. The length of stride he took to do this, is noted, and it should be pointed out that this is *all* the stride he needs to deliver the pitch. The coach should then back up, and allow the pitcher to follow the same procedure, demonstrating to him how he is thrown off balance when he strides too far.

8. Chest on Knee Drill. (Illustration number six page 84)

This drill is used to help the pitcher who does not bend his back in the delivery. As in most of the drills the action is exaggerated to emphasize the proper techniques.

Procedure. The pitcher is instructed to touch his chest to his front knee as he delivers the ball. This drill may be combined with drill number five.

9. Palm Facing Up Drill. (Illustration number seven page 84)

This drill is used to aid maximum arm and wrist action and a full follow-through. It is a great aid to the pitcher who does not get his hand on top of the ball but pushes the ball with his hand in back of it. As the pitcher finishes his motion he concentrates on following through with his pitching hand fully bent with the palm facing up.

10. Holding Wrist Drill.

This drill is used for several purposes. It is used to strengthen the hand and wrist in the lead ball drill, and to practice the various rotations, by isolating the hand and finger action. One of the most important aspects of throwing breaking pitches is the finger action. Through this drill, finger action and finger dexterity can be emphasized.

Procedure. The pitcher holds his pitching wrist with the opposite hand. He throws the ball into a mattress or pillow using only the action of the hand and fingers. His concentration must be upon applying the proper rotation to the ball.

11. Hand To Hand Drill.

This drill is used for the same purpose as drill number ten.

Procedure. The pitcher practices his rotation by rotating the ball from his pitching hand to his other hand, concentrating on the spin.

12. Ten Foot Drill.

The purpose of this drill is to practice throwing the breaking pitches with proper rotation.

Procedure. If the pitcher is having trouble with his curve ball, for example, he should practice imparting the rotation from a distance of ten feet and gradually move back. This is a good drill that can be used in the pitcher's home. The pitcher can get his father to catch the ball for him at this short distance, which probably would not be possible from the regular distance.

13. Clawing Drill.

This drill is primarily used to increase the action on the pitcher's fast ball. The emphasis is upon increasing the finger action on the ball.

Procedure. The pitcher grips the ball according to his regular fast ball grip and literally squirts the ball out of his hand by applying pressure on top of the ball with his index and middle fingers. After doing this, using the hand to hand drill, he should practice pitching from the regular distance emphasizing the clawing action. The pitcher should be able to hear the ball whistle, if it is clawed properly.

14. T.V. Drill.

The T.V. drill is used to develop finger action on the curve ball. Its name is derived from the fact that it can be practiced while watching television.

Procedure. With the arm in proper curve ball position (high elbow, wrist in) the pitcher repeatedly clicks his index and middle fingers on his thumb as he rotates his arm at the shoulder, using the curve ball techniques described in chapter six.

MENTAL DRILLS

The mental drills are designed to help the pitcher meet difficult situations under stress. They are used to expose the pitcher to different types of pressure in practice situations, so that he will be better able to operate efficiently under fire in the actual games. Do not expect your pitcher to come through under fire if he has never been exposed to pressure. You must be aware of the level of development of each of your pitchers so that these drills will not tend to discourage him unduly. There are five drills of this type.

15. Live Stopper Drill.

This drill is designed to see how a pitcher reacts under pressure in a relief situation. It can be used both as a screening device and as a device to help your staff adjust to the pressure-filled relief situation.

Procedure. Four or five pitchers are kept warm, as they would be for relief duty. The pitcher is called in from the bull pen to perform a certain duty. You can set up any type situation for him that you wish. He is given only one try to succeed. No second chances! The rest of your ball club is used as live offense and defense. Below are some of the situations that might be used:

1. Bases loaded, winning run on third, none, one, or two out.
   A. Protect against the squeeze play.
   B. Protect against the fly ball.
   C. Force the batter to hit the ball on the ground for the double play.
   D. Protect against ground ball to the opposite side of the infield.
   E. Come in with two balls on the batter.
2. Winning run on second, no outs.
3. Winning run on first, no outs.
4. Bunt situations.

Any situation may be set up to suit your particular needs. This is also good practice for the rest of your team.

16. Game Situation Drill.

This drill is designed to give the pitcher experience in pitching under game conditions.

Procedure. The pitcher pitches for a certain number of outs. If you want to pitch him three innings, he will pitch them consecutively, rather than in half inning stints. The pressure must be as near actual game pressure as possible, in order to achieve the desired results. This drill may be speeded up and varied, by assuming that every batter has a one and one count, or any other assumed count that you might wish to set up.

17. Pressure Drill Through the Strings.

This drill is used mainly to improve the pitcher's control in stressful situations.

Procedure. The pitcher puts pressure on himself by simulating pitching to actual hitters while throwing through the strings. He should have a knowledge of the weaknesses of the next team he will pitch against and pitch to these weaknesses as he goes through the line-up, hypothetically. He should also put himself in different situations (drill number fifteen) and pitch his way out of them. The emphasis should be upon control and thinking how, why, what, and where, he is going to throw each pitch. *Concentration* is what he is striving for.

18. Coach's Pressure Drill.

This drill is designed to force the pitcher to think and pitch in a pressure situation on the spur of the moment.

Procedure. While the pitcher is engaged in regular practice throwing to the catcher, the coach comes up behind him and sets up a hypothetical pressure situation on the spur of the moment. By doing this the pitcher is kept on his toes in practice and learns to think and act quickly. You might come up behind the pitcher and say, "Jones is up, the count is three and two, the bases are loaded, two outs, and the winning run on third, pitch!" You will feel the pressure mount as the pitcher must deliver.

19. Assumed Pressure Drill.

This drill is used to get the pitcher in tone for the game. You have undoubtedly seen a pitcher get "blasted" in the first inning and heard people say that he did not warm up properly. There is more to warming up than the fifteen or twenty minutes spent in physical warmup. The pitcher must also warm up mentally. He must not go out to the mound in the first inning just then awakening to the fact that he is in the middle of a battle. He must be prepared ahead of time. This drill is used for mental preparatory purpose.

Procedure. When the pitcher is warmed up physically and has several minutes left before he finishes his warmup he should set up several of the hitters he is going to face and imagine some hypothetical pressure situations and pitch his way out of them. If he does not feel ready between innings he can tone himself by pitching to the first hitter hypothetically.

FIELDING DRILLS

The pitcher must be drilled repeatedly on defensive fundamentals so that he will be able to react without hesitation during the game. During the actual game the pitcher only has a split second in which to react to a defensive situation. These situations must be understood and practiced over and over so that the pitcher can react automatically.

20. Multi-Purpose Drill.

This drill is divided into three defensive plays that the pitcher is often called upon to execute. These plays include covering first with no men on, getting the double play or force at second on a bunt, slow roller, or hard hit ball, and getting the force at third on a slow hit ball or bunt down the third base line. Refer to chapter ten for the specific techniques and methods of executing each one of these plays.

Procedure. This drill should be practiced ten minutes every day. The drill fits neatly into the practice schedule when used at the beginning of practice after everyone is properly warmed up. While the infielders and pitchers are engaged in the drill, the outfielders can be getting ready to throw in or can be working on their individual drills. The pitchers are stationed behind, and to the right of the mound, each one with a ball. The first pitcher takes his position on the rubber and throws the ball to the catcher. As the ball crosses the plate the coach fungoes the ball so that the first baseman fields it and the pitcher covers first. Each pitcher in turn follows the same procedure. This part of the drill may be varied by hitting balls that the pitcher must field and throw to the first baseman covering first.

The second part of the drill is started in the same manner except that the pitcher must attempt to get the force-out or double play at second base. All types of balls should be fungoed, slow rollers, line drives, hard ground balls, *etc.* Remember, the catcher directs the pitcher on this play, and on hard hit balls the pitcher automatically throws to second, unless the ball is fumbled or the catcher yells otherwise.

In the third part of the drill the ball is fungoed so that the third baseman and pitcher must make a decision on the play, as explained in chapter ten. The third baseman either fields it and throws to first or second, or allows the pitcher to field it as he covers third. These three drills, once they are understood, should take no longer than ten minutes of the practice schedule.

21. Back-Up Drill.

The back-up drill is used for the purpose of helping the in-fielders and pitchers work together in blocking bad throws and recovering balls that get by the infielder. Five minutes spent on this drill, each day, will pay large dividends.

Procedure. The pitcher stations himself, approximately twenty-five feet behind the infielder covering the base. A coach or manager positions himself about twenty feet in front of the infielder and delivers various type throws to him that are hard to handle. The infielder attempts to block the throws and the pitcher acts as the back-up man as he would in a game.

22. Back-Up Positioning Drill.

This drill is used to help the pitcher anticipate which base to back up as explained in chapter ten. It affords the pitcher actual practice in making the split second decision as to which base to back up.

Procedure. The pitcher takes his position on the rubber ready to pitch. The coach yells out any of the situations, such as, runner on first and a hit to the outfield, and the pitcher reacts accordingly. The drill can also be accomplished by having live runners and letting the pitcher adjust according to where the coach fungoes the ball. It is recommended that both these variations of the drill be used.

23. Runner's Mistake Drill.

This drill is used to get the pitcher in the habit of watching the runners for any tell-tale signs that he is going to steal. He should also be checking the runner to see if he is leaning, jumping, walking, or in any other way putting himself in a position where he might be picked-off.

Procedure. The pitchers are lined up behind the mound to wait their turn. Each pitcher stays on the rubber until three runners have had a chance to steal second base. The runners deliberately make mistakes or "telegraph" when they are going to steal. When the pitcher picks up one of these tell-tale signs he attempts to pick the runner off first. The runners do not make these mistakes on every pitch. If the pitcher feels the runner is not going and does not detect any mistakes he throws to the plate. The coach must very carefully evaluate the pitcher's techniques and advise him when he misses one of the runners give-away signs or mistakes.

24. Defense Against Offensive Situations.

The purpose of this drill is to give the pitchers practice in meeting the various offensive plays. Included in this drill are the various pick-off plays, the defense against the squeeze and the defense against the double steal. (The methods of presenting these plays are explained in chapter ten.)

Procedure. This drill is organized so that all the plays and defenses can be practiced in fifteen minutes (after they are learned and understood). The pitchers are lined up near the mound and take their turn on the rubber as in the other drills. To begin the drill, runners are placed at first and second and the pick-off plays at second and at first are practiced. The runners rotate from first to second and then back to first. Next, the runners are placed at first and third and the coach stations himself in the dugout to give offensive signals (they must be changed so that the pitchers do not know them). The regular steal, the delayed steal, or the double steal can be signaled for, and the pitcher and defense must then act accordingly. The runners rotate from first to third and back to first. In the last part of the drill the runners are stationed at third and the defenses against the squeeze and the steal of home are practiced. This entire drill can be completed in fifteen minutes.

CONDITIONING DRILLS

Getting in proper condition to pitch is hard work and is certainly not one of the most interesting aspects of pitching. For a pitcher to get in top condition he must push himself beyond the point where it begins to "hurt." There is no easy way to get into condition, but the running should be made as interesting as possible to get more out of the pitcher. These drills have been selected because of the contribution they make toward getting the pitcher in shape and the variety they add to the conditioning program. (See chapter three for details on the conditioning program.)

25. Pick-Up Drill.

The purpose of this drill is to get the pitcher to move quickly from side to side and to field slow rolling balls.

Procedure. The pitchers pair off, one acting as the tosser and the other as the fielder. The fielder stations himself approximately ten yards from the tosser. The tosser rolls the ball first to one side and then to the other side of the pitcher. The ball should be thrown so that the pitcher can barely reach it each time. Upon fielding the ball it is returned to the tosser and the fielder keeps fielding the ball until he has fielded fifty of them. When he has fielded fifty chances cleanly, he changes places with the tosser.

26. Football Pass Drill.

The purpose of this drill is to increase endurance and to get the pitcher's legs in shape.

Procedure. Each pitcher is stationed on the left field line, with a ball. The coach is positioned in center field. Each pitcher, in turn, sprints to the coach, tosses him the ball and continues sprinting toward right field to catch the ball thrown by the coach. The coach should try to throw the ball in such a manner that the pitcher must go all out to catch it. The drill continues from the right field line toward the left, etc., until each pitcher has caught twenty throws.

27. Fungo Drill.

The purpose of this drill is to increase endurance and to get the pitcher's legs in shape.

Procedure. The pitchers line up in single file on the left field line. Each one in turn sprints toward centerfield to catch the ball, fungoed off the bat of the coach. The coach should try to lead the pitcher so that he will have to go all out to catch the ball. After attempting to catch the ball, the pitcher jogs to the right field line to await his return trip to left field. Each pitcher must catch, or make a good effort to catch, twenty balls to complete the drill.

28. Ball Return Drill.

The purpose of this drill is to get the pitcher to move quickly and to bend over to field ground balls. This drill is harder than it appears at first, and is a very good conditioning drill.

Procedure. Five balls are placed at ten yard intervals for fifty yards, as on a football field. The pitchers line up behind the starting line, ten yards from the first ball. At the command go, the first pitcher sprints to the first ball, picks it up, sprints back to the starting line, puts it down, sprints to the second ball, sprints back to the starting line, puts it down, etc., until all five balls are placed at the starting line. The pitcher then picks up a ball, sprints to the fifty yard mark, places it down, sprints back to the starting line, picks up the next ball, places it on the forty yard mark, etc., until all the balls are back in their original places. To add competition to the drill the total time to perform the drill should be timed and records kept.

29. Running the Bases for Time.

The purpose of having the pitchers run the bases for time is to help them get in condition using an activity that is close to game conditions.

Procedure. The pitchers line up in single file at home plate and one at a time sprint to second base (by way of first). After all have run from first to second, they are lined up again and are timed running from second to home. Running two bases instead of four is used because you can get more out of a pitcher if he runs short distances, and then rests, and runs again. The drill ends when the pitcher has made five complete cycles at full speed. The accumulative time for the five cycles is posted in the locker room for motivation.

30. Runners in Game Situation Drill.

The purpose of this drill is to get the pitcher's legs in condition by running the bases in the regular game situation drill.

Procedure. In this drill the team is stationed in their regular defensive positions. The pitchers act as runners and the coach fungoes the ball simulating actual game conditions. The pitchers must run the bases at top speed, as they would in a regular game.

31. Twenty Yard Sprint Drill.

The purpose of this drill is to get the pitcher's legs in condition by sprinting short distances.

Procedure. The pitcher sprints twenty yards and walks ten yards alternately, for ten complete lengths of the football field.

32. Twenty Yard Continuous Running Drill.

This drill is usually used at the very end of practice to put the finishing touches on the day's conditioning.

Procedure. The pitchers sprint back and forth over the twenty yards without stopping for three minutes and then rest for one minute and repeat the drill.

33. Rabbit Drill.

The purpose of this drill is to add variety to the conditioning grind. It is a very competitive drill and is excellent for building endurance and strengthening the pitcher's legs.

Procedure. The pitchers line up as near as possible, according to speed, the fastest ones in front, etc. The first pitcher stations himself about ten feet down the first base line facing first base. The next pitcher stands at home plate, facing first, ready to chase the first pitcher. At the command, both runners sprint for second (by way of first). If the second pitcher catches the first before he reaches second base, the first pitcher must come back and become the chaser and the second pitcher goes to the back of the line. If the second pitcher does not catch the first before he reaches second base, the pitcher goes to the end of the line and the second pitcher is again the chaser. Fresh pitchers keep moving up in the line competing against the last loser. The drill continues until all pitchers have been through the line at least twice.

Index

211